Shakespeare's Tragedies: A Very Short Introduction

VERY SHORT INTRODUCTIONS are for anyone wanting a stimulating and accessible way into a new subject. They are written by experts, and have been translated into more than 45 different languages.

The series began in 1995, and now covers a wide variety of topics in every discipline. The VSI library now contains over 500 volumes—a Very Short Introduction to everything from Psychology and Philosophy of Science to American History and Relativity—and continues to grow in every subject area.

Very Short Introductions available now:

Available soon:

For more information visit our website

www.oup.com/vsi/

Stanley Wells

# SHAKESPEARE'S TRAGEDIES

## A Very Short Introduction

OXFORD
UNIVERSITY PRESS

# OXFORD

UNIVERSITY PRESS

Great Clarendon Street, Oxford, OX2 6DP,
United Kingdom

Oxford University Press is a department of the University of Oxford.
It furthers the University's objective of excellence in research, scholarship,
and education by publishing worldwide. Oxford is a registered trade mark of
Oxford University Press in the UK and in certain other countries

Published in the United States of America by Oxford University Press
198 Madison Avenue, New York, NY 10016, United States of America

British Library Cataloguing in Publication Data

Data available

Library of Congress Control Number: 2016962490

ISBN 978-0-19-878529-3

Printed in Great Britain by
Ashford Colour Press Ltd, Gosport, Hampshire

# Contents

# List of illustrations

1. Shakespeare between the Two Muses of Comedy and Tragedy (1825). Richard Westall (1765–1836), oil painting.

# Introduction: what is a tragedy?

People like labels. When we think about plays there's a natural tendency to group them into categories according to their subject matter and the way in which it is treated. The commonest dramatic categories are tragedy and comedy, terms which refer to the plays' overall tone and substance, and we may subdivide them respectively into domestic tragedies, heroic tragedies, and love tragedies; or into romantic comedies, farcical comedies, and sentimental comedies; and so on. Putting it simplistically, by comedies we mean plays that aim to make us laugh and that have a more or less happy ending—often marriage—and when we speak of tragedies we mean plays that end unhappily, usually with the death of one or more of their central characters.

Around half of Shakespeare's thirty-seven or so plays are tragedies in the most basic sense of the word, that is to say, plays leading up to the death of their central character or characters. He wrote them throughout his career, interspersing them with other plays that are primarily comic in tone. No doubt he varied the categories partly because, at least after the first few years when he worked as a freelance, in 1594 he became the house dramatist of a single company of actors, the Lord Chamberlain's, later the King's Men, who would expect him to provide variety of entertainment for playgoers who would often pay repeated visits to the same

1

playhouse—though it was also because he responded to internal as well as external pressures, seeking to deepen his exploration in dramatic form of matters of life and death. Hamlet, for example, is far more self-questioning than Romeo; Macbeth's career of self-destruction is portrayed with more inwardness than Richard III's; and Lear's descent into madness is charted with more psychological plausibility than Titus Andronicus's.

In this book I shall devote a chapter to each of the plays generally classed as tragedies, in the order in which Shakespeare wrote them, except for those classed in the Folio as histories, which will form the subject of a separate volume. In keeping with the aims of this series, I hope to be genuinely introductory—that is, to assume readers who, while they may have heard of some or all of these plays, have had no close experience of them either on the page or on the stage—and also to give readers a sense of why it's worth taking an interest in them. I shall write about each play's plot and structure, its origins, its literary and theatrical style, its place in Shakespeare's development, its impact, and the opportunities and challenges it has offered to performers over the centuries.

In 1623 the compilers of the first collected edition of plays by Shakespeare, known as 'the First Folio', grouped the plays not simply as comedies and tragedies, but as comedies, histories, and tragedies. Under 'histories' they included only plays that tell stories based on English history; those based on Greek, Roman, Scottish, and ancient British history—all of which end with the deaths of one or more of their central characters—they called tragedies. They found it difficult to pigeonhole certain plays. Although *Cymbeline*, normally regarded nowadays as a comedy (if of a rather peculiar kind), has historical elements, they printed it among the tragedies; and they squeezed in *Troilus and Cressida*, which Bart van Es, in his volume in the Very Short Introduction series devoted to the comedies, discusses as a 'problem comedy', between the histories and the tragedies.

The Folio's overall grouping of the plays is illogical in that two of its categories—tragedies and comedies—refer to dramatic form, whereas the other, histories, refers to subject matter. In 1598 the first published list of plays by Shakespeare had, more logically, recognized only two categories: comedies and tragedies. This is in *Palladis Tamia—'The Treasury of the Muses'*—by Francis Meres, who wrote:

> As Plautus and Seneca are accounted the best for comedy and
> tragedy among the Latins, so Shakespeare among the English is the
> most excellent in both kinds for the stage; for comedy, witness his
> *Gentlemen of Verona*, his *Errors*, his *Love Labour's Lost*, his *Love's
> Labour's Won*, his *Midsummer Night's Dream*, and his *Merchant of
> Venice*: for tragedy his *Richard the 2, Richard the 3, Henry the 4,
> King John, Titus Andronicus* and his *Romeo and Juliet*.

There is a puzzle here: no play called *Love's Labour's Won* exists; it may be lost, or perhaps it was an alternative title for a play that survives. But that is by the by. What is relevant to discussion of Shakespeare's tragedies is that Meres lists under this heading plays relating to events of English and Roman history (along with the non-historical *Romeo and Juliet*) that the Folio hives off under the separate category of histories. In other words Meres is categorizing plays by their form, as derived from classical drama, whereas the Folio prints separately certain plays that dramatize historical events whether or not these plays shape the events they tell into stories that are primarily tragic or comic in tone.

This categorization—grouping some plays by their form, others by their subject matter—has permanently—and in my opinion regrettably—affected discussion of them. The events of history can be dramatically represented in a variety of ways; to give examples only from Shakespeare, he shapes the events of the reigns of Richard II and Richard III into the form most obviously associated with tragedy, culminating in the death of a central character, but he dramatizes the happenings of the reigns of

3

Henry IV and Henry V over three plays which include the death of Henry IV but do not make this a climactic event, which include many complexly comic episodes involving Shakespeare's most famous comic character, Sir John Falstaff, and which culminate not, as we should expect in a tragedy, with the death of Henry V but, as in a comedy, with his successful wooing of the Princess of France and with the hope of unification of their two kingdoms.

It is also worth remembering that most of Shakespeare's comedies include elements that may be considered to be tragic in nature—near-rape of a heroine in *The Two Gentlemen of Verona*, the death threats that hang over Egeon in *The Comedy of Errors*, over Antonio in *The Merchant of Venice*, over Claudio in *Measure for Measure*, and over Prospero in *The Tempest*, and the apparent deaths of Hero in *Much Ado About Nothing*, of Hermione in *The Winter's Tale*, and of Innogen in *Cymbeline*, to give only a few examples. The genre—or sub-genre—of tragi-comedy was developing during the later part of Shakespeare's career, and he adopted some of its conventions.

Just as Shakespeare's comedies often verge on tragedy, so his tragedies frequently offer a wittily ironic perspective on the action such as is provided by Aaron the Moor in *Titus Andronicus* and by the Fool in *King Lear* as well as other elements associated with comedy such as the satire on the citizens in both *Julius Caesar* and *Coriolanus*, the Porter in *Macbeth*, and the clowns in *Othello* and *Antony and Cleopatra*. And *Hamlet* is shot through with comedy almost from start to finish. This suggests that when Shakespeare set about looking for a story to dramatize he was more concerned to find one that offered possibilities for variety of dramatic effect than for one that would fit neatly into the traditional kinds of drama. No one has expressed this more eloquently than Samuel Johnson when he wrote, in the 1765 Preface to his edition of Shakespeare,

Shakespeare's plays are not in the rigorous and critical sense either tragedies or comedies, but compositions of a distinct kind; exhibiting the real state of sublunary nature, which partakes of good and evil, joy and sorrow, mingled with endless variety of proportion and innumerable modes of combination; and expressing the course of the world, in which the loss of one is the gain of another; in which, at the same time, the reveller is hasting to his wine, and the mourner burying his friend; in which the malignity of one is sometimes defeated by the frolick of another; and many mischiefs and many benefits are done and hindered without design.

Is it possible, nevertheless, to arrive at a more precise definition which would distinguish tragedies from plays that simply have unhappy endings? As a dramatic form tragedy originated in Ancient Greece with the work of writers such as Sophocles, Euripides, and Aeschylus, whose practice was famously defined in a treatise known as *The Poetics*, by Aristotle (385–322 BC), which has had a profound influence on later thought. Aristotle considered that all plays should obey the so-called unities of time, place, and action, and that tragedies should depict the downfall of heroic figures as the result of circumstances leading to a reversal in their fortunes causing their death. This supposedly led to a catharsis, or purging, of pity and terror in the spectator. (Though there is no evidence that Shakespeare had read Aristotle, the point in *King Lear* at which Albany, calling for the dead bodies of Goneril and Regan to be brought before him, says 'This justice of the heavens, that makes us tremble, / Touches us not with pity' (*King Lear*, 5.3.226–7) may seem to invoke the Aristotelian notion of catharsis.)

In Shakespeare's time, as in ours, the word 'tragedy' could be applied in a very broad sense outside the drama, to events that had disastrous consequences for those who endured them, and to narrations, whether dramatic or not, of such events. Certainly, however, Shakespeare knew about tragedy as a dramatic form. We cannot be sure that he knew any of the great tragedies of classical antiquity at first hand, but he was certainly aware of, and influenced by, their derivatives, the Roman tragedies of Seneca (*c*.4 BC–AD 65), which had been translated into English by Jasper Heywood and others and published in 1581, five years after the building of the first important London playhouse—the Theatre. Seneca's plays, deadly serious, full of sensationalism, intended to be recited or read rather than acted, rhetorical, moralistic, and bombastic, full of accounts of horrible deeds and often featuring ghosts and witches, exerted an enormous influence in their printed form (not through performance) on the first great wave of Elizabethan dramatists, such as Thomas Kyd, Christopher Marlowe, George Peele, and Robert Greene, and, partly through their work, on their slightly later contemporary and immediate successor, Shakespeare.

Seneca is one of the only two playwrights of any period mentioned by name anywhere in Shakespeare's writings—the other is the comic dramatist Plautus (*c*.254–184 BC), whose plays, along with those of his successor Terence (*c*.190–159 BC), were taught, and even performed, in the grammar schools of Shakespeare's time. In *Hamlet* Polonius names Seneca and Plautus as typical of the extremes of tragic and comic writing—'Seneca cannot be too heavy, nor Plautus too light' (*Hamlet*, 2.2.401–2). Interestingly, these are the dramatists with whom, only two or three years before Shakespeare wrote *Hamlet*, the literary chronicler Francis Meres had compared Shakespeare himself (as discussed earlier).

Certainly some of Shakespeare's plays reflect a knowledge of classical practice. His most classically derived play has the word 'comedy', Roman in origin, in its title: *The Comedy of Errors* is based on Plautus's *Menaechmi* (*The Menaechmus Twins*) and obeys (more or less) the so-called classical unities of place, time, and action—meaning that the action is limited to a single plot enacted in a single location over only one day. (The other play in which Shakespeare comes close to this is *The Tempest*.) Even here, however, Shakespeare complicates the story by adding a plot based on a medieval romance which he was to use again towards the end of his career in one of his least classically constructed plays, *Pericles*.

Shakespeare uses the words 'tragedy' and 'tragic' in his writings a number of times, but always with a very general sense of, as the classic *Shakespeare Lexicon* by Alexander Schmidt puts it, 'a dramatic representation of a serious action' or 'a mournful and dreadful event'. In fact what may be his first 'representation of a serious action' is in non-dramatic form. This is his long narrative poem *The Rape of Lucrece*, published in 1594 as a companion piece to the wittily comic (though ultimately elegiac) *Venus and Adonis* of 1593. Both poems tell classically derived stories based on poems by the Roman poet Ovid, one of Shakespeare's favourite writers to whom he refers, and whom he quotes, many times throughout his career.

*Lucrece* relates the tragic tale of the rape of this Roman matron by Tarquin, a close friend and fellow-warrior of her husband Collatine, and of her consequent suicide. Lucrece is the tragic victim, but the poem's portrayal of the tormented state of mind and inner struggles to withstand temptation of her ravisher, driven by lust to betray her husband whom he calls 'my kinsman, my true friend' (l. 237), bestows on Tarquin the status of a later tragic hero such as Macbeth, who imagines 'withered murder' moving towards his victim 'with Tarquin's ravishing strides' (*Macbeth*, 2.1.52–6). Lucrece, bemoaning her fate, makes a theatrical reference as she invokes 'Night, image of hell, … Black stage for tragedies and murders fell', lines which would have reminded Shakespeare's readers of the black stage hangings used for tragic plays and referred to in the first line of *Henry VI*, Part One: 'Hung be the heavens with black'—in a playhouse of the time 'the heavens' referred to the canopy over the stage.

In amplifying Ovid's tale, relatively brief in its original telling, Shakespeare resorts to frequent use of '*sententiae*', moral statements commenting on the action which help to give dignity and high seriousness to his dramatic tragedies, too. These plays have features in common which may help us to know what Shakespeare understood by 'tragedy'. All of them end in the death of one or more of the central characters; all, like *Lucrece*, contain a certain amount of moral commentary and philosophical reflection (but then, so do his comedies.) But when we have said this we start having to make exceptions, saying for example 'all of them—except *Romeo and Juliet* and *Othello*—are set in the more or less distant past', or 'all of them—except *Romeo and Juliet* again, and perhaps *Othello*—focus on high-born characters whose fate involves national destiny.'

This has caused some critics to despair of ever defining what Shakespeare meant by tragedy, so that for example the critic Kenneth Muir said, in a British Academy lecture of 1958, 'There is no such thing as Shakespearian tragedy. There are only Shakespeare's tragedies.' This statement, though attractively terse—and quotable—is perhaps a little glib. Wide-ranging and varied in effect though Shakespeare's tragedies are, most of them portray one or more central characters with a degree of inwardness and with a suggestion that the disasters leading to their downfall are inextricably bound up with their personalities. (*Romeo and Juliet* is perhaps an exception (again), in that here the lovers' fate seems to be determined rather by external forces than by their own characters.) The same is true, however, of characters in some of his plays written in comic form, most notably Angelo in *Measure for Measure* and Leontes in *The Winter's Tale*, even though they are eventually redeemed. The Folio's categorization is reflected in the fact that in this series of Very Short Introductions the plays are divided into its three groupings. For this reason, writing on the tragedies, I shall limit myself to those that are not based on English history.

It is the absence of a definable theory of tragedy in Shakespeare plays that go under this label that encourages me to write about each play individually rather than adopting a thematic approach. In doing so I hope to give a sense of each play's uniqueness, of what makes it enjoyable and meaningful to readers and playgoers today, of the influence that it has exerted, and the pleasure that it has given.

# Chapter 1

# Tragedies on the stages of Shakespeare's time

Tragedies were immensely popular at the time Shakespeare came on the theatrical scene. The brightest star among his early contemporaries, and probably the only one who, had it not been for his death at the age of 29 in 1593 when Shakespeare was still a relative beginner, might have grown into a serious competitor, was Christopher Marlowe. Born only a couple of months before Shakespeare, and like him of humble birth, Marlowe, a university graduate, was an earlier developer; a great lyric poet and translator; and a prolific dramatist whose two-part play *Tamburlaine the Great* of 1587 was both a sensational success with audiences and a seminal influence on his contemporaries and successors.

Marlowe followed this with other great tragedies, including the heavily ironic *The Jew of Malta*, the daringly innovative *Edward II*, based on English history and telling of the disastrously homosexual love of the King for his favourite, Piers Gaveston, and the serio-comic *Dr Faustus*, all of which also exerted a demonstrable influence on Shakespeare's style and dramaturgy. Ben Jonson, in his great tribute to Shakespeare printed in the First Folio of 1623, was to write of 'Marlowe's mighty line', paying tribute to his mastery of the heroic style that was only one of his many contributions to the development of English drama.

Shakespeare also learnt much from the less prolific Thomas Kyd (1558–94), whose Seneca-influenced *The Spanish Tragedy*, written about 1587, is the first of a long line of English tragedies centred—like Shakespeare's *Titus Andronicus* and *Hamlet*—on revenge. Like *Hamlet*, written some fifteen years later, Kyd's play features a revenge plot, a ghost, mad scenes, dumb shows, a thwarted love affair, a play within the play staged by the revenger, a philosophical concern with the afterlife, and episodes of violence which culminate in a maelstrom of murder. Written almost entirely in highly patterned verse with long rhetorical speeches, including passages of Latin, some directly quoted from Seneca, and Italian, and riddled with classical allusions, it might seem likely to have been above the heads of ordinary playgoers, yet it was highly popular both in print, with ten editions between 1592 and 1633—more than any of Shakespeare's plays—and on the stage, and was frequently parodied and imitated. The line 'Hieronimo go by, go by' became a catchphrase of the Elizabethan theatre, and the soliloquy in which Hieronimo grieves over the loss of his murdered son, Horatio, was frequently quoted and—to some degree, affectionately—parodied. Its rhetorical, highly patterned style is close to that adopted by Shakespeare in his earliest plays.

> O eyes!—No eyes, but fountains fraught with tears;
> O life!—No life, but lively form of death.
> O world!—No world, but mass of public wrongs,
> Confused and filled with murder and misdeeds!
> O sacred heavens! If this unhallowed deed,
> If this inhuman and barbarous attempt,
> If this incomparable murder thus
> Of mine, but now no more my son,
> Shall unrevealed and unrevengèd pass,
> How should we term your dealings to be just,
> If you unjustly deal with those that in your justice trust?
> (*The Spanish Tragedy*, 3.2.1–11)

But it also features sensational action, not least the moment when Hieronimo deliberately bites off his own tongue.

The form and style of Shakespeare's tragedies, as of all his plays, were determined in part by the physical conditions of the playhouses within which they were to be acted, by the nature of the companies that performed them, the conventions of dramatic presentation obtaining at the time, and to a lesser extent by the expectations of those who went to see them. Early in his career, at least, audiences expected plays to be written largely or wholly in verse, and that most of this would be blank verse—the ten-syllabled, unrhymed iambic line made popular for drama by Marlowe. Romeo's 'But soft, what light from yonder window breaks...' is such a line. Rhyme, however, often breaks in, especially for instance as a way of rounding off a speech, a scene, or a play:

> It is concluded. Banquo, thy soul's flight,
> If it find heaven, must find it out tonight.

says Macbeth after giving instructions for Banquo's murder (*Macbeth*, 3.1.142–3).

Shakespeare uses prose with increasing freedom, and for varied effect, as time goes on. Only four of his plays, all histories, are written entirely (or almost entirely) in verse (*Richard II, King John*, and the first and third of the plays on the reign of Henry VI). For much of his career, plays were written in far more varied literary styles than those of later periods, ranging from elaborately literary verse to colloquial prose. At no other period in the history of English drama has so much of the most sophisticated literature of the time been composed for the theatre. Individual speeches would often have qualities which we associate with operatic arias, expanding or even holding up the action while characters react, emotionally or intellectually, to what is happening to them. The best-known example is Hamlet's 'To be or not to be...' (*Hamlet*, 3.1.58) Even prose speeches, both serious and comic, would often be written in a highly conventionalized, rhetorical style influenced by the training in rhetoric and oratory offered by Elizabethan grammar schools.

Plays were acted continuously—act intervals were introduced only late in Shakespeare's career. Performances in public playhouses would be given in the open air, and consequently before nightfall. These playhouses typically had stages that thrust into the auditorium, with two or three doors allowing entrances from the backstage area, or tiring ('attiring') -house; an upper playing level; and above this a canopy that could hold flying equipment and a throne that could descend from above. Fireworks could stand in for lightning, sound effects could be provided by, for instance, the rolling of cannon balls down a trough to simulate thunder, and cannon could even be fired to serve as a royal salute, as they disastrously were during a performance of *All is True, or Henry VIII*, in 1613 when they ignited the thatch and burned the theatre to the ground.

Companies would employ musicians to provide accompaniment for dances and marches, trumpeters for fanfares, drummers for battle scenes, and some of the actors would be expected to sing—as, for instance, Ophelia, Desdemona, and Lear's Fool do—and to accompany themselves on a lute. There was no curtain to separate the audience from the players, so at the ends of plays the stage had to be cleared, bodies to be removed: *Hamlet, King Lear*, and *Coriolanus* all end with a funeral procession.

Performances also took place in the halls of royal palaces and, especially when the companies were on tour in the provinces, in guildhalls (as they did in Stratford-upon-Avon during Shakespeare's boyhood), in great houses, in inns and inn-yards, and in improvised conditions which might require reduced resources and rapid adjustments to play-texts if, for example, there was no upper level for Juliet's appearance at her window; or stage aperture for Ophelia's grave. Play texts during this period had to be fluid.

13

Audiences were accustomed to dramatic and theatrical conventions beyond the regular use of verse which may be unfamiliar to modern audiences. Plays might open with an introductory prologue, as *Romeo and Juliet* and *Troilus and Cressida* do; or be punctuated by Chorus speeches, as are *Henry V* and *Pericles*; or, like *As You Like It* and *The Tempest*, end with an epilogue. Characters frequently spoke in soliloquy—long speeches, usually in verse, addressed either to themselves or to the audience: among the most familiar today are Hamlet's 'To be or not to be...' (*Hamlet*, 3.1.58) and Macbeth's 'Tomorrow, and tomorrow, and tomorrow...' (*Macbeth*, 5.5.18). They often spoke aside—to selected onstage characters, or to the audience.

Acting companies usually had around fourteen full-time actors who could be supplemented by part-time extras; an actor would often play more than one role in a single performance, and playwrights needed to take account of this by, for example, allowing time for costume changes. One major difference from later practice is that all female roles, even older women's parts, such as Lady Macbeth and Cleopatra, were taken by male actors, ranging from young boys—some of whom had been trained in choir schools or by senior actors in the adult companies—up to late teenagers: this helps to explain why there are relatively few female roles in the plays—only two in *Julius Caesar* and in *Hamlet*, for instance—and why most of these are young, rather than older women.

It is difficult to generalize about the audiences of the time. They may have included ill-behaved groundlings, capable of 'nothing but inexplicable dumb-shows and noise' as Hamlet puts it (*Hamlet*, 3.2.12–13), but before we patronize them we should remember that they applauded and made popular some of the most sophisticated and emotionally and intellectually demanding plays ever written—as we shall see in the following pages.

# Chapter 2
## *Titus Andronicus*

*Titus Andronicus*—the least highly regarded and the most
obviously dated of all Shakespeare's plays—nevertheless has fine
passages and offers opportunities for great acting. It is also
Shakespeare's most Senecan play, the first of the tragedies not to
be based on English history, and probably the first of all. Although
it is set in Ancient Rome, it is the least genuinely historical of the
Roman plays. Its first recorded performances were at the Rose
playhouse, on Bankside, in 1594, and it was printed in the same
year (with no indication of who wrote it) and went through two
further editions before appearing with an additional scene (3.2) in
the 1623 First Folio.

It was a great popular success in its own time, as we can see from
Ben Jonson's sneering, and perhaps envious remark in the Preface
to *Bartholomew Fair* (1614) that 'He that will swear *Jeronimo*
[an alternative title for *The Spanish Tragedy*] or *Andronicus* are
the best plays yet shall pass unexcepted at here, as a man whose
judgement shows it is constant and hath stood still these five and
twenty or thirty years.' Later, however, it came to be regarded as
a terrible mistake, at least until a landmark production by Peter
Brook, starring Laurence Olivier, in 1955, released previously
unsuspected areas of greatness in the text.

People have often found the play's presentation of horrific events so distasteful that they have suspected, and indeed hoped, that Shakespeare wrote either none or (as is probably true) only part of it. Nevertheless, Francis Meres listed it among Shakespeare's plays in 1598 and his colleagues included it as his in the First Folio of 1623. A dramatist called Edward Ravenscroft (c.1654–1707) said it was 'the most indigested and incorrect piece in all his works'; and that it seemed 'rather a heap of rubbish than a structure.' He said he'd heard that Shakespeare had only given 'some master touches to one or two of the principal parts or characters'; even so he thought it was worth adapting the play for the theatres of his time. His criticism and his doubt about its authorship have persisted throughout the centuries. In an essay first published in 1927, T. S. Eliot wrote of it as 'one of the stupidest and most uninspired plays ever written.' Since then, however, a number of great productions with magnificent performances in the title role, along with new ideas about the artistic validity of representing violence on the stage, have brought about a revaluation of the play. Most scholars have come to accept the view that Shakespeare wrote it in collaboration with George Peele, who is generally credited with the first act along with 2.1 and 4.1. This does not mean that Shakespeare would have dissociated himself from the play—it may have been a perfectly happy partnership—and it still leaves him responsible for some extremely nasty sequences of action.

Although the play is set in Ancient Rome, its story is not based on recorded history. Its double revenge plot is artfully devised to incorporate a large number of horrifying but theatrically effective, and sometimes deeply moving, episodes, written mostly in highly rhetorical blank verse. The spectacular opening draws heavily on the resources of the Elizabethan theatre as Roman tribunes and senators march on to the upper level to the accompaniment of trumpets and drums. To them enter below at one side of the stage Saturninus, elder son of the late emperor of Rome, and at the other side the younger son, Bassianus, each accompanied by as many followers as the theatre could muster. Trumpeters and drummers add to the effect. The two leaders are in competition for 'the imperial diadem of Rome' with the veteran warrior Titus, who makes an impressive entry in his chariot with his four surviving sons, Martius, Mutius, Lucius, and Quintus along with his daughter Lavinia and the black-covered coffins of as many of his other twenty-one sons, all killed in battle, as the theatre can muster. He has brought them back to Rome for burial, and somehow a tomb opens to accommodate the coffins.

In Titus's train are the captive Tamora, Queen of the Goths, her three sons, and a Moor, Aaron, who, however, says nothing and plays no part in the action of the long opening scene. Titus orders the ritual slaughter of Tamora's eldest son, Alarbus, in appeasement for the death of his own sons, and he is hauled off to be sacrificed, off stage. Titus, pleading age, yields his claim to the throne to Saturninus, who announces first that he will marry Lavinia but then switches his attentions to Tamora and marries her, whereupon Bassianus marries Lavinia. The first revenge action gets under way as Tamora incites her sons, the appalling Chiron and Demetrius, first to stab Bassianus to death (on stage) and then to drag off his wife Lavinia to 'satisfy their lust' on her. Later they bring her back on stage in one of Shakespeare's most chilling stage directions: *'Enter the Empress's sons, Chiron and Demetrius, with Lavinia, her hands cut off, and her tongue cut out, and ravished.'* They chuck Bassianus's body into an onstage pit, and fix the blame on two of Titus's sons, who are tricked into falling into the pit and condemned to die.

Aaron, Tamora's lover, deceives Titus into thinking he can save his sons' lives by allowing his hand to be chopped off, as it is, on stage. A messenger brings back Titus's hand along with the chopped-off heads of his two sons, 'in scorn to thee sent back.' This provokes a vow of revenge followed by a grisly procession of departure:

> The vow is made. Come, brother, take a head,
> And in this hand the other will I bear.

> And Lavinia, thou shalt be employed.
>
> Bear thou my hand, sweet wench, between thine arms.
>
> (3.1.278–81)

The second revenge action opens with an emblematic scene (3.2) that appears to be a late addition (possibly written by Thomas Middleton): it was not printed until the Folio of 1623. In it Marcus kills a fly. Titus rebukes him but when Marcus pleads that 'it was a black ill-favoured fly, / Like to the Empress' Moor' stabs repeatedly at it. Lavinia uses the stumps of her arms to turn the pages of a copy of Ovid's *Metamorphoses* to the tale of the rape of Philomela, and then to manipulate a staff with which she writes the names of her rapists in the sand on which she stands.

Tamora has had a baby by Aaron and, because it is black, wants him to kill it, but he refuses and later kills its nurse (on stage). Titus, virtually insane, dispatches messengers to the gods to plead his case. In the closing scenes, driven to madness, along with his brother Marcus and his last surviving son, Lucius, he achieves a spectacular final sequence of revenge upon Tamora and her sons, killing his own daughter so that she may not 'survive her shame', cutting the throats of Tamora's sons (on stage), and serving up to Saturninus and Tamora a pie in which he has baked their heads. Within the space of three lines of text—a few seconds of stage action—he stabs Tamora to death, is himself killed by Saturninus, and is revenged by his son's killing of Saturninus. Lucius becomes Emperor and is left with Marcus to bury the dead, to punish Aaron, and to re-establish order in Rome.

Presented in summary fashion, the play's action may seem ludicrous. Indeed it has often provoked inappropriate laughter. In 1923, the theatre critic James Agate wrote that the audience laughed when the deaths of Tamora, Titus, and Saturninus followed each other within about five seconds, as in a burlesque melodrama.

At the other extreme, some parts of the play have seemed overwritten. When Marcus comes upon his raped and mutilated niece Lavinia, instead of calling for help, as might have been expected in a naturalistic drama, he delivers a forty-seven-line blank verse speech elegantly written in an Ovidian style and with direct references to the classical legend of the rape of Philomela on which it is based. It includes the lines:

> Why dost not speak to me?
> Alas, a crimson river of warm blood,
> Like to a bubbling fountain stirred with wind,
> Doth rise and fall between thy rosèd lips,
> Coming and going with thy honey breath.
> But sure some Tereus hath deflowered thee
> And, lest thou shouldst detect him, cut thy tongue.
> Ah, now thou turn'st away thy face for shame,
> And notwithstanding all this loss of blood,
> As from a conduit with three issuing spouts,
> Yet do thy cheeks look red as Titan's face
> Blushing to be encountered with a cloud.
> Shall I speak for thee? Shall I say 'tis so?
> O that I knew thy heart, and knew the beast,
> That I might rail at him to ease my mind!
>
> (2.4.21–35)

This speech, full of similes and metaphors, alliterations and conventional epithets, classical allusions (some deriving from Ovid), and rhetorical questions (they have to be rhetorical as the tongue-less Lavinia cannot speak) is consciously artificial writing, imitative of the classical writers whose work the young Shakespeare would have studied at school not all that long before he helped to write the play.

Naturalistically, the problem is that poor Lavinia is in urgent need of practical help, not of having poetry made out of her situation. Peter Brook, in the play's first really great post-Elizabethan production, of 1955, with Laurence Olivier as Titus, omitted the whole of this speech. All the same, the great literary critic Frank Kermode was wrong to say that Marcus 'is making poetry about the extraordinary appearance of Lavinia, and making it exactly as he would if he were in a non-dramatic poem.' This is an untheatrical reading of the text. In fact the verse shows Marcus to be conscious of the silent presence of the raped and mutilated woman, addressing her directly, giving cues for her reactions, and allowing for poignant pauses as she gestures or moves in response to what her uncle says. Julie Taymor, in her 1999 film, shortens the speech but shows awareness of the problem by causing Marcus to approach Lavinia from afar (easier on film than on stage), only slowly realizing what has happened to her. And in a landmark production by Deborah Warner of 1987 the actor playing Marcus delivered the speech in hushed tones so that it became a deeply moving attempt, enacted as it were outside time, to master the facts, and thus to survive the shock, of a previously unimaginable horror.

To say this is to say that modern directors need to help audiences to overcome difficulties of understanding which arise from the out-of-date conventions in which the play is written. But it is also true that the play includes great passages of poetic drama which can be opened up by actors capable of plumbing the depths of the play's rhetoric, some of it expressed in words of harrowing simplicity, and by speaking it in a manner that reveals depths of suffering akin to those experienced by some of Shakespeare's greatest tragic characters such as Macbeth and King Lear. Laurence Olivier, wrote the theatre critic J. C. Trewin, began by portraying Titus as a grizzled old warrior, and then 'was able to move out into a wider air, to expand him to something far larger than life-size, to fill stage and theatre with a swell of heroic acting', finding greatness in the simple phrase 'I am the sea' (3.1.224); and Brian Cox, in the Deborah Warner production, conveyed ever-increasing intensity of suffering up to the mirthless laughter with which he preceded the devastatingly simple line, 'Why, I have not another tear to shed' (3.1.265). Warner even succeeded in avoiding a comic response to the play's final sequence of horrors by tactful stage direction—but here it has to be admitted that she was helping the playwrights out rather than realizing unsuspected dramatic potential in the text.

# Chapter 3
## *Romeo and Juliet*

'In fair Verona where we lay our scene' says the Prologue to this popular play, and if you go to Verona today you will see much evidence that this still fair city appreciates the compliment. In the courtyard of what the city authorities have designated as Juliet's house you can stare at a balcony said to be hers, touch the naked breasts of a statue of her, send emails to her about your love life (they will be answered by volunteers), post love letters on the walls, and of course buy souvenirs of your visit. Further afield you can even make a pilgrimage to what is said to be her tomb.

The story of the 'star-crossed lovers', as the Prologue calls them, was already popular when Shakespeare wrote his play, around 1595, basing its narrative fairly closely on a long poem (by Arthur Brooke, who drowned young in a shipwreck soon after writing it) which had been first published over thirty years earlier and which itself recycled an already popular story. It has become one of the world's great love stories, and has continued to gain in popularity, in other plays and in films, operas, ballets, orchestral music, and in numerous retellings and variants, in some of which the lovers become an elderly or a same-sex couple. Its greatest literary and theatrical incarnation is in Shakespeare's play.

The difference between *Titus Andronicus* and *Romeo and Juliet*, written only a few years apart, is a measure at once of the speed of

Shakespeare's development as both a dramatist and a poet and of the openness of his concept of tragedy, which in this play permits the inclusion of romance and of many comic elements. The play is carefully structured as a double tragedy of love. As the term 'star-crossed' suggests, this tragedy results rather from fate or the influence of external forces than from faults and tensions within the characters themselves, as in some of Shakespeare's other tragedies. It's an 'if only' kind of tragedy—if only Juliet had accompanied Romeo when he went into banishment; if only the letter telling Romeo that Juliet has taken a sleeping potion had not gone astray; if only Juliet had woken from her apparent death a few minutes earlier...

The play's plot, based on the tragic consequences of the feud between 'two households, both alike in dignity'—the Montagues, to which Romeo belongs, and the Capulets, Juliet's family—is laid out with exceptional care. The action takes place over only five days. In the opening scenes we see dangerous conflict between the servants of the two families, portrayed with rough, bawdy humour in a street fight, which helps to establish the play's concern with sex and violence. It is quelled by the first appearance of the Prince of Verona, establishing him as a figure of authority and power. The theme of romantic love is introduced by Benvolio's account of how Romeo has been moping around alone in the early morning, avoiding his friends, and then shutting himself up in love-sick seclusion. The woman he loves at this stage of the play, Rosaline—who never appears—will have nothing to do with him; Romeo's love is in the mind, not the body.

Cheering up a bit, he and his friends gatecrash a torch-lit ball in the house of his family's enemies, the Capulets, to which Juliet, aged not quite 14, belongs. He is smitten with love for her as soon as he sees her—'O, she doth teach the torches to burn bright!'—and now love-in-the-head is enriched with sexual longing. They talk, they kiss chastely, he learns who she is from her Nurse, Juliet speaks of loving him: 'My only love sprung from my only hate!',

23

and later he sees her looking out of a window (not on a balcony, as is often said):

> But soft, what light from yonder window breaks?
> It is the east, and Juliet is the sun.
> Arise, fair sun, and kill the envious moon,
> Who is already sick and pale with grief
> That thou, her maid, art far more fair than she.
>
> (2.1.44–8)

The waning 'moon' is, metaphorically, the unresponsive (and absent) Rosaline. Unseen by Juliet, Romeo overhears her expressing love for him, makes himself known, and they plight their troth in some of the most rapturously lyrical yet also delicately humorous poetry in the English language. 'O swear not by the moon, th'inconstant moon', says Juliet,

> That monthly changes in her circled orb,
> Lest that thy love prove likewise variable.
>
> (2.1.152–3)

To which Romeo, momentarily nonplussed, replies 'What shall I swear by?'

Their rapture is briefly overshadowed by foreboding:

> Well, do not swear. Although I joy in thee,
> I have no joy of this contract tonight.
> It is too rash, too unadvised, too sudden,
> Too like the lightning which doth cease to be
> Ere one can say it lightens.
>
> (2.1.158–62)

Romeo consults a Friar who agrees to marry them and does so, returns to his friends, and becomes involved in another brawl in which his friend Mercutio, the Prince's kinsman, is killed by

Juliet's cousin Tybalt. As Mercutio dies, he blames the fight on the
family feud: 'A plague o'both your houses!' The play's tone
darkens. Romeo fights and accidentally kills Tybalt, and is
banished by the Prince in his second intervention in the action.

Juliet, not knowing of the fight, speaks a rapturous soliloquy in
which, declaring her fully sexual longing for Romeo, she calls on
night to teach her how to 'lose a winning match / Played for a pair
of stainless maidenhoods'—both lovers are sexually inexperienced.
Her Nurse brings news of Romeo's banishment to nearby Mantua;
Romeo, seeking help from the Friar, becomes distraught and tries
to kill himself; the Friar encourages him to visit Juliet before
leaving the city; Juliet's parents propose an arranged marriage
with a young nobleman, Paris; and Romeo and Juliet, having
consummated their marriage in their first—and, as it will turn out,
only—night of love, say farewell in another exquisitely, sensuously
poetic but also gently humorous duet.

JULIET:  Wilt thou be gone? It is not yet near day.
    It was the nightingale, and not the lark,
    That pierced the fear-full hollow of thine ear.
    Nightly she sings on yon pom'granate-tree.
    Believe me, love, it was the nightingale.
ROMEO:  It was the lark, the herald of the morn,
    No nightingale. Look, love, what envious streaks
    Do lace the severing clouds in yonder east.
    Night's candles are burnt out, and jocund day
    Stands tiptoe on the misty mountain tops.
    I must be gone and live, or stay and die.

                                        (3.5.1–11)

In the later stages of the action, Juliet, to her father's fury, resists
his plan to marry her off to Paris, and the Friar, in a distinctly
hare-brained scheme, persuades her to take a sleeping potion
which will cause her parents to think she has died and to inter her

in the family vault, while he will arrange for Romeo to ride back from Mantua and to rescue her when she recovers from the effects of the potion. But the Friar's letter to Romeo goes astray and Romeo arrives at the vault, finds Paris there and kills him in a duel, and, believing Juliet really to have died, takes poison and kills himself. The Friar finds the bodies of Romeo and Paris just before Juliet wakes, runs away when he hears someone coming, and Juliet, seeing Romeo dead, kisses his lips, snatches up his dagger, and kills herself with it.

In a final stretch of action, the Prince is called to the scene, the Friar returns, the lovers' parents arrive, and the Prince calls on the Friar—the only person who is in the know about what has happened—to offer an explanation, which he does and, saying 'I will be brief', delivers a lengthy summary of the entire plot—justified because much of it comes as news to his on-stage listeners. Finally the Prince points out to the heads of the families that the lovers' deaths are a punishment on their feud, and they shake hands and offer to raise golden statues to the lovers' memory. The Prince rounds off the play with lines which distance its action from us as its fiction recedes into the past. They take the form of the sestet—the final six lines—of a sonnet:

> A glooming peace this morning with it brings.
>> The sun for sorrow will not show his head.
> Go hence, to have more talk of these sad things.
>> Some shall be pardoned, and some punishèd;
> For never was a story of more woe
> Than this of Juliet and her Romeo.

(5.3.304–9)

The play's scenario is cunningly devised so that it incorporates a variety of theatrical entertainment: fights, duels, a dance, love scenes, virtuoso set speeches, a scene of mourning, and a double death scene. Nevertheless this is a very literary play and a long one, with around 3,100 lines of verse and prose. The dialogue draws on a wide range of literary forms. Its prologue is a sonnet, with all the associations of romantic literature that this would have carried for contemporary audiences; so is the shared dialogue in which the lovers first meet, and other passages of the play employ versions of the form too. But it also encompasses an exceptionally wide range of other literary styles, in both prose and verse, and this is in part responsible for the richness of its characterization.

The rough and vigorous prose of the servants, filled with bawdy wordplay, counterpoints brilliantly with the romantic though often delicately humorous lyricism of the lovers. Although Juliet's Nurse speaks inconsequentially, rambling from one topic to another as she reminiscences about Juliet's childhood, she does so within a verse structure that its author has cunningly controlled to give an impression of a lack of intellectual control in the speaker:

> Even or odd, of all days in the year
> Come Lammas Eve at night shall she be fourteen.
> Susan and she—God rest all Christian souls!—
> Were of an age. Well, Susan is with God;
> She was too good for me. But, as I said,
> On Lammas Eve at night shall she be fourteen,
> That shall she, marry, I remember it well.
> 'Tis since the earthquake now eleven years,
> And she was weaned—I never shall forget it—
> Of all the days of the year upon that day,
> For I had then laid wormwood to my dug,
> Sitting in the sun under the dovehouse wall.

> (1.3.18–29)

Romeo's close friend Mercutio—in modern productions their relationship is sometimes interpreted as homoerotic—speaks in a wittily yet bawdily fantastic style that calls to mind, especially in his 'Queen Mab' speech (*Romeo and Juliet*, 1.4.55–94), the delicate poetry of Oberon and Titania in *A Midsummer Night's*

*Dream* (written either just before or just after this play); the blank verse of Friar Laurence, on the other hand, is typically measured and controlled.

*Romeo and Juliet* has been accused of being over-literary: the 19th-century actor-manager Sir Henry Irving—who admittedly was a great butcher of texts—described it as 'a dramatic poem rather than a drama', and this point of view has been reflected in its treatment on stage and even more so on film. The dialogue encompasses much intricate wordplay, resembling that which Shakespeare was using around this time in comedies such as *Love's Labour's Lost* and *The Comedy of Errors*, sometimes difficult for modern readers and audiences to follow. There is an oddly experimental use of, apparently, overlapping dialogue in the reactions of Juliet's parents and her Nurse to her seemingly dead body (Figure 2) (*Romeo and Juliet*, 4.4.50–91). And the musicians, who have been hired to play at the aborted marriage,

2. Drawing of the Nurse attempting to waken Juliet from her drugged sleep (*Romeo and Juliet*, 4.4.28). John Massey Wright (1777–1866), watercolour.

speak or sing fragments of popular songs as the company disperses, with a touchingly serio-comic effect. (The episode is often omitted in modern performance in a way that reduces the experimental diversity of Shakespeare's writing in this highly original play.)

All this makes for a text that, for all its richness, has over the centuries often been shortened and even adapted in performance. The play's closing scenes have proved especially problematic. The 17th-century dramatist Thomas Otway incorporated into a new play called *Caius Marius* (1780) a version of the death scene of *Romeo and Juliet* in which, apparently thinking that Shakespeare had missed an opportunity by failing to give his lovers a closing conversation, he caused the heroine to wake up before her lover expired, and gave them a touching duologue.

This was adapted by the great 18th-century actor David Garrick in a version of the play more closely based on Shakespeare in which the lovers have a melodramatic final conversation likely to seem to a modern reader ludicrously out of key with the rest of the play. 'Bless me, how cold it is!' says Juliet on waking, and later, 'And did I wake for this!' Nevertheless it has the advantage of giving the actor playing Romeo a stronger death scene than Shakespeare provides, and was hugely popular for well over a century. Bernard Shaw, writing in 1894, described his first experience of seeing the play, 'in which Romeo instead of dying forthwith when he took the poison, was interrupted by Juliet, who sat up and made him carry her down to the footlights, where she complained of being very cold, and had to be warmed by a love scene, in the middle of which Romeo, who had forgotten all about the poison, was taken ill and died.' No modern director would be likely to incorporate Garrick's dialogue into the text, but in many productions, on stage and on film, the terrible irony of the situation has been pointed by compressing the dialogue and by causing Juliet to show signs of life as Romeo dies.

Although the final line of the Prologue speaks of the 'two hours' traffic of our stage', that can scarcely have been true even in Shakespeare's time, when it would have been comparatively simply staged. In modern performance it is regularly shorn of 600 or 700 lines, with consequent telescoping of parts of the action.

The highly literary quality of this play might appear to suggest that it is more suitable for reading than for performance, and certain passages, above all the famous 'balcony' scene, with its idealized expressions of the raptures of first love, have a detachable quality that has made them popular on the printed page; but the fact that many of the literary conventions and devices that the play employs—the quibbles and puns, the classical references, the elaborate series of verbal misunderstandings such as those between the Nurse and Juliet when the Nurse brings news of Tybalt's death but Juliet thinks she is speaking of Romeo (*Romeo and Juliet*, 3.2.36–68), the repetitions of the extraordinary—by any standards—scene of keening over Juliet's supposedly dead body (4.4.50–91)—are likely to be unfamiliar to the untrained modern reader—all this means that this play even more than most is likely to be best approached through performance, whether on the stage or in one of the several, variously attractive film versions, which include the visually beautiful but heavily abbreviated one directed by Franco Zeffirelli of 1968 and the radically and wittily updated *Romeo + Juliet* of 1996, directed by Baz Luhrmann with Leonardo di Caprio and Claire Danes as the lovers.

Inevitably film directors adapt and abbreviate the text—as to a lesser extent do theatre directors—but they are able to mediate it in ways that render it more approachable by modern audiences. A major change in practice since Shakespeare's time is of course the casting of female actors in the women's roles. With boys playing both Romeo and Juliet, Shakespeare was unable to represent love-making in anything like a realistic way, which is why on their wedding night we only see the lovers as they are about to part; modern productions regularly set this scene in a bedroom and employ varying degrees of undress to suggest what has gone on before the farewells.

The diversity and richness of Shakespeare's prose and verse in this play create great opportunities for virtuoso performances from actors able to realize its potential. In particular the role of Mercutio incorporates complex comedy which verges on tragedy in his death scene, and his counterpart, Juliet's Nurse, played in a classic series of performances by Dame Edith Evans in which a theatre critic described her as being 'as earthy as a potato, as slow as a carthorse, and as cunning as a badger', has become one of the great female roles of the Shakespearian repertoire. It is often said that no actress can ever hope to look young enough to play Juliet—who is repeatedly stated to be not quite 14—while having the technical skill to do justice to what she has to say, and the role of Romeo does not offer its interpreters as wide a range of opportunities as Shakespeare's other great tragic roles. Nevertheless *Romeo and Juliet* is both a unique dramatic and literary masterpiece and a measure of the variety with which Shakespeare handles the concept of tragedy.

# Chapter 4
## *Julius Caesar*

Many tragedies of Shakespeare's time, both before and after he wrote, are concerned with the fall from power, and the eventual death, of great men of the past. And in writing a play about the assassination of Julius Caesar, perhaps the greatest ruler who had ever lived, and a major historian, Shakespeare was dramatizing one of the most famous events in the history of the world. He based his play quite closely on the life of Caesar in the great (and highly readable) *Lives of the Noble Grecians and Romans* by the Greek-Roman historian Plutarch in a translation into English (via French) of 1579 by Sir Thomas North, dedicated to Queen Elizabeth, which he was to draw on heavily also for his other plays based on Roman history. But as usual he felt free to remould the facts to suit his dramatic purpose, for instance by compressing into a single stretch of action in the Forum scene (3.2) events that occurred in several different places over the space of some six weeks.

In doing so he wrote a study of the uses and abuses of political power, the morality of rebellion and even of assassination, which would have been easily applicable to the state of the nation at the time it was first performed, at the Globe in 1599, when Queen Elizabeth I was inevitably coming towards the end of her long reign. The play has struck answering chords at, especially, times of political crisis in many later ages and in relation to many different situations, both national and personal. This has made it amenable to productions that update the action, or change its location, so that it gains in topical and local relevance. Orson Welles's Mercury Theatre, New York, production of 1937 adapted the play as anti-Fascist propaganda in which Cinna the poet died at the hands, not of the Roman crowd, but of a Secret Police Force; a Stratford-upon-Avon production by Gregory Doran in 2012, played without an interval by an all-black cast, relocated the action to a tyrannical regime in Central Africa.

The play is described in the First Folio, where it first appeared in print, as *The Tragedy of Julius Caesar*. Caesar, who dies half way through the action, has one of the smaller roles; he is however the dominant force even after his death, and his ghost appears, briefly, in the later part of the play. The conspirators Cassius and Mark Antony have longer roles which give more scope for virtuoso acting, especially in Mark Antony's rhetorical swaying of the citizens in his 'Friends, Romans, countrymen' (3.2.74–106); but the principal tragic character may be regarded as Brutus, whose suicide forms the climax of the play, evoking Mark Antony's tribute 'This was the noblest Roman of them all.'

With only two female characters, Calpurnia and Portia, whose roles are small, the play as conceived offers little opportunity for women actors, but in 2012 an all-female production directed by Phyllida Lloyd, set in a women's prison, at the Donmar Warehouse in London with Harriet Walter as Brutus, redressed the gender balance. In Shakespeare's time it would have been acted by a relatively small company of male actors, but in more recent times the opportunities for spectacle afforded by the crowd scenes have been exploited on both stage and film.

What is still the best film, made as early as 1953 and directed by Joseph L. Mankiewicz, uses an almost uncut text and has a remarkable cast including Marlon Brando as Mark Antony, James Mason as Brutus, and John Gielgud—who had played the role successfully on stage—as Cassius. Like other cinematic versions this retains the historical setting, aided by 1,200 toga-clad extras, while subtly suggesting parallels with Mussolini and Hitler.

At the time Shakespeare wrote the play he had already referred to Caesar as both emperor and historian several times.

> That Julius Caesar was a famous man:
> With what his valour did t'enrich his wit,
> His wit set down to make his valour live.
> Death made no conquest of this conqueror,

says the young Prince Edward in *Richard III* (3.1.84–7). In *Love's Labour's Lost* a letter from Don Adriano de Armado quotes Caesar's most famous saying, '*Veni, vidi, vici*'—'I came, I saw, I conquered' (4.1.67)—also quoted in two later plays—and in *Richard, Duke of York* (3 *Henry VI*) Queen Margaret, speaking of the Prince's death at the hands of King Edward, Richard and Clarence, says:

> They that stabbed Caesar shed no blood at all,
> Did not offend, nor were not worthy blame,
> If this foul deed were by to equal it.
>
> (5.5.52–4)

Caesar's blood, spilt by the conspirators, was to figure prominently in Shakespeare's play about him.

Like *Romeo and Juliet* (after its prologue), *Julius Caesar* opens in mid-stream and with a bang as Murellus and Flavius, tribunes of the people—officers elected, like trade union officials, by the plebeians from among themselves to protect their own interests—berate the citizens, who are taking time off work 'to see Caesar, and to rejoice in his triumphs.' Vividly the tribunes ask if the workmen are so ungrateful as to have forgotten Pompey, the great warrior and statesman who had married Caesar's daughter by his first wife but had been defeated by Caesar and later killed in battle. They order the men to remove the trophies with which they have decked images on the route to the Capitol. Crucially, they express the fear that unless Caesar's wings are clipped he will become an all-powerful tyrant:

> These growing feathers plucked from Caesar's wing
> Will make him fly an ordinary pitch,
> Who else would soar above the view of men
> And keep us all in servile fearfulness.

> (1.1.72–5)

Caesar's power is already under threat, and in the following scene, where he first appears, this becomes more apparent. He is presiding over the public games celebrating a religious feast, and asks his henchman Mark Antony, who is 'stripped for the course'—that is, ready to run naked (historically, if not in the theatre), as was the custom—to touch his wife Calpurnia in the superstitious belief that this will relieve her barrenness and enable her to conceive a child. Already there is a hint of vulnerability in Caesar, and this is augmented when the voice of a soothsayer emerges from the crowd with a warning that Caesar should 'beware the Ides [the 15th] of March'—in other words that disaster is likely to befall him on that date. When Caesar and his train leave to watch the games, two leading statesmen, Brutus and Cassius, remain behind.

In a circumspect conversation Brutus lets it be known that he has been troubled with thoughts that he is unwilling to reveal, Cassius encourages him to unburden himself, and when they hear offstage shouts indicating that the people are acclaiming Caesar as King, Cassius embarks upon a lengthy speech in which he sardonically mocks Caesar's human weakness, declaring that:

> [ … ] this man
> Is now become a god, and Cassius is

> A wretched creature, and must bend his body
> If Caesar carelessly but nod on him.
>
> (1.2.117–20)

When more shouts show that 'new honours' are 'heaped upon Caesar', Cassius returns to the attack with another long piece of impassioned oratory beginning:

> Why, man, he doth bestride the narrow world
> Like a Colossus, and we petty men
> Walk under his huge legs, and peep about
> To find ourselves dishonourable graves.
>
> (1.2.136–9)

He calls on Brutus to join him in taking their fate into their own hands and overthrowing Caesar.

The Machiavellian way in which Cassius works on the relatively innocent Brutus resembles that in which, in a later tragedy, Iago will work on Othello. Brutus, still cautious, admits that he feels sympathy with what Cassius says while refusing to commit himself irrevocably to the cause.

> What you have said
> I will consider. What you have to say
> I will with patience hear, and find a time
> Both meet to hear and answer such high things.
>
> (1.2.168–71)

When Caesar, looking angry, returns with his followers he expresses suspicion of Cassius:

> Yon Cassius has a lean and hungry look.
> He thinks too much. Such men are dangerous.
>
> (1.2.195–6)

He is astute in his suspicion; but also, in a subtle piece of characterization, Shakespeare shows Caesar's personal vulnerability as he says to his ally Mark Antony:

> Come on my right hand, for this ear is deaf,
> And tell me truly what thou think'st of him.
>
> (1.2.214–5)

These opening episodes have set up a situation in which Antony is clearly allied with Caesar, Cassius is opposed to him, and Brutus is undecided. They have done so in a way that draws upon Shakespeare's classical education in its use of rhetoric and the skills associated with oratory, skills that he had deployed with conspicuous success but to different ends in the war scenes of *Henry V*, written shortly before this play. The Roman workmen have spoken in prose, but the patricians so far use verse which can rise to great eloquence, as it does in Cassius's attempts to sway Brutus against Caesar.

Caesar's accounts of his campaigns, known as his *Commentaries*, are written in the third person, and Shakespeare adopts this for some of his speeches in the play, creating an impression of aloof dignity, even pomposity:

> Caesar should be a beast without a heart
> If he should stay at home today for fear.
> No, Caesar shall not...
>
> (2.2.42–4)

And Shakespeare skilfully varies the tone and style of his dialogue as he represents the individual voices of the conspirators. Cassius has most difficulty in persuading Brutus, who ultimately is not only deceived by Cassius's rhetoric but uses rhetoric in arguing himself into a frame of mind in which he decides to do something he knows to be wrong:

> It must be by his death. And for my part
> I know no personal cause to spurn at him,
> But for the general. He would be crowned.
> How that might change his nature, there's the
>     question.
>
> (2.1.10–13)

In other words, Caesar is to be killed for a crime he has not yet committed. And when it comes to the point of execution, Brutus himself again uses rhetoric in a manner that suggests self-deception, trying to dress up an inglorious deed in noble words:

> Let's be sacrificers, but not butchers, Caius.
> We all stand up against the spirit of Caesar,
> And in the spirit of men there is no blood.
> O, that we then could come by Caesar's spirit,
> And not dismember Caesar! But, alas,
> Caesar must bleed for it. And, gentle friends,
> Let's kill him boldly, but not wrathfully.
> Let's carve him as a dish fit for the gods,
> Not hew him as a carcass fit for hounds.
>
> (2.1.166–74)

God-meat or dog-meat, the end result for Caesar will be the same.

Brutus's lack of self-knowledge is still more apparent in his efforts to glorify the deed after it is done:

> Stoop, Romans, stoop,
> And let us bathe our hands in Caesar's blood
> Up to the elbows, and besmear our swords;
> Then walk we forth even to the market-place,
> And, waving our red weapons o'er our heads,
> Let's all cry 'peace, freedom, and liberty!'
>
> (3.1 106–11)

As the conspirators obey him Shakespeare breaks the time barrier
of the historical past to draw out the emblematic significance of
what they are doing:

CASSIUS: How many ages hence
   Shall this our lofty scene be acted over,
   In states unborn and accents yet unknown!
BRUTUS: How many times shall Caesar bleed in sport,
   That now on Pompey's basis lies along,
   No worthier than the dust!
CASSIUS: So oft as that shall be,
   So often shall the knot of us be called
   The men that gave their country liberty.

(3.1.112–19)

The irony is both powerful and blatantly obvious.

The most eloquent displays of rhetoric in the play come in the
Forum as first Brutus, then Mark Antony address the Roman
people over Caesar's dead body. Brutus speaks in laconically
effective prose which stirs the crowd to enthusiasm: 'Live, Brutus,
live, live!—bring him with triumph home unto his house—Give
him a statue with his ancestors.' But he has made two serious
miscalculations, both of them against the counsel of the more
worldly-wise Cassius: first, by arguing against killing Mark
Antony along with Caesar; and, secondly, by allowing him to
speak to the crowd, as he does with surpassing eloquence in the
great speech beginning 'Friends, Romans, countrymen, lend me
your ears...'.

Having worked up the crowd to a frenzied desire for vengeance,
using rhetoric of action, as he uncovers Caesar's body, as well as of
words, he unleashes them to 'fire the traitors' houses' with the
chilling words:

> Now let it work. Mischief, thou art afoot.
>
> Take thou what course thou wilt.
>
> (3.2.253–4)

And before long the first great sweep of the play's action, brilliantly moulded by Shakespeare into dramatic form out of the relatively unshaped historical narrative, comes to a climax with the senseless killing of Cinna the poet, a symbolic figure of innocence whose occupation leads him to use words in a search for truth rather than, as the conspirators have done, to cloak the truth.

If you're seeing the play on stage there may well be an interval here, though some directors follow Elizabethan practice in dispensing with one altogether, moving straight into the scene in which the triumvirate of Mark Antony along with two characters we have not seen before, Octavius Caesar and Lepidus, cold-bloodedly plan their campaign against Cassius and Brutus. The subsequent quarrel between the latter two went down especially well with the play's earliest spectators, causing one of them—Leonard Digges—to write, in lines first printed in the 1623 Folio,

> So have I seen, when Caesar would appear,
> And on the stage at half-sword parley were
> Brutus and Cassius; O, how the audience
> Were ravished, with what wonder they went thence,
> When some new day they would not brook a line
> Of tedious though well-laboured *Catiline*
>
> [a tragedy by Ben Jonson].

This scene has continued to be popular especially for the opportunities it gives to the actors playing Cassius and Brutus, and in general the later part of the play is more effective on stage than on the page. Shakespeare shows the spirit of Caesar still at work by making his ghost appear briefly to Brutus (Figure 3) in a carefully devised episode to tell him 'Thou shalt see me at Philippi'. The play's closing scenes depict the working out of

3. Caesar's ghost appears to Brutus in his tent (*Julius Caesar*, 4.2).
William Blake: water-coloured pen and ink drawing, 1806.

Caesar's posthumous vengeance on his killers in the battle, at which Cassius, falsely believing that all is lost, has himself killed by his servant, Pindarus, and Brutus dies on his own sword declaring:

> Caesar, now be still.
> I killed not thee with half so good a will.
> (5.5.50–1)

Antony and Octavius have triumphed, but the play comes to a muted conclusion as Antony speaks his tribute over Brutus's body:

> This was the noblest Roman of them all.
> All the conspirators save only he
> Did that they did in envy of great Caesar.
> He only in a general honest thought
> And common good to all made one of them.
> His life was gentle, and the elements
> So mixed in him that nature might stand up
> And say to all the world 'This was a man'.
> (5.5.67–74)

They are fine words, recalling Brutus's:

> I know no personal cause to spurn at him,
> But for the general ...
> (2.1.11–12)

But we, remembering the efforts with which Brutus had to persuade himself to the rebels' cause, may feel we know him better than Antony did.

# Chapter 5
## *Hamlet*

It's difficult for anyone to avoid *Hamlet* altogether. 'To be or not to be, that is the question' is among the world's most-quoted phrases, whether in English or in translation. The image of a handsome, fit young man looking into the empty eye sockets of a human skull—Hamlet and Yorick, live young Prince and dead clown—is an endlessly reproduced emblem of the human condition (Figure 4). And 'something is rotten in the state of Denmark' is frequently applied to situations very different from that for which it was coined. What's more, the play's basic story has been endlessly adapted, reshaped, and re-imagined in many different media—film, television, opera, ballet, works of visual art, travesties and burlesques, comic books, and so on—with the result that it may well have crossed the consciousness of people who have neither read nor seen it, and are never likely to do so.

But what exactly is *Hamlet*? By comparison with, for example, *Julius Caesar* and *Macbeth*, which have come down to us only in single versions, the very words of the play are curiously fluid. The first printed text, of 1603—known as the bad quarto—has only about 2,200 lines and is probably a corrupt version of what Shakespeare wrote ('To be or not to be—ay, there's the point', Hamlet says); the second, of 1604, has about 3,800 lines, while the version printed in the First Folio, of 1623, is about 230 lines

4. Hamlet with Yorick's skull. From the Gower Memorial, Bancroft Gardens, Stratford-upon-Avon.

shorter and lacks Hamlet's last soliloquy, but also includes about seventy new lines and differs verbally at many points. And the version you are likely to read in a modern edition may well be a composite text drawing on all three of the early printings and containing passages that are almost always omitted in performance.

The play's textual fluidity is a measure of the flexibility of works of dramatic art in general. Plays are far more variable than, for instance, paintings or sculptures, and *Hamlet* is even more variable—and therefore subject to a wider range of interpretation—than most. It is different every time it is acted—different not only, like all plays, because of the varying physique, age, and personality of the actors, the design of the set and costumes, and all the other variables that affect any transition from page to stage, but also in plot and dialogue.

There are for instance many film versions, which offer differing selections from any printed text. Franco Zeffirelli's abbreviation of 1990 with Mel Gibson as the Prince lasts about two and a quarter hours, and both adds episodes and reassigns speeches, whereas Kenneth Branagh's, of 1996, in its full form lasts for four hours and twenty minutes. (An abbreviated version also appeared, demonstrating anxiety that the full text might be too much for some spectators.) Though every version has the same basic central story of Hamlet's revenge for his father's murder, each of them inevitably presents a more or less subtly different narrative, some of them omitting whole scenes and even such a major thread of the original as the story involving Fortinbras and the invasion of Denmark, ending the play abruptly with Hamlet's death. All this helps to explain why the play, and its central character, have been subject to an exceptionally wide range of interpretation. Still, some things about it are constant if we read or see it in any reasonably faithful version.

It is no accident that the most familiar image of the play is the one pictured in this chapter—that of a living person contemplating a skull. If the play has one overriding theme, it is that of how people react to death. At its start, in the arresting opening scene, we see the ghost of 'the king that's dead.' Prince Hamlet's father appears horrifyingly but speechlessly at midnight on the battlements of a castle in Denmark, so far with no apparent purpose, to a group of men who include Hamlet's friend Horatio. They go off to tell Hamlet what they have seen, confident that 'this spirit, dumb to us, will speak to him.'

Then, in a vividly contrasting ceremonial court scene, Hamlet makes his first appearance, conspicuously dressed in mourning black, and stands silent while Claudius, brother of the dead King, speaks of his marriage to his recently deceased brother's widow, Gertrude, sends messengers to deal with a threat to the kingdom from young Fortinbras of Norway, and goes on ignoring the silent Hamlet while granting a request for leave of absence from Laertes, son of his chief courtier, the elderly Polonius.

When at last Claudius and Gertrude turn their attention to the Prince it is to rebuke him at great length for continuing to grieve for his father's death and to refuse permission for him to return to university at Wittenberg.

Left alone, Hamlet, in the first of the soliloquies for which the role is famous, contemplates bringing about his own death:

> O that this too too solid flesh would melt,
> Thaw, and resolve itself into a dew,
> Or that the Everlasting had not fixed
> His canon 'gainst self-slaughter!
>
> (1.2.129–32)

His grief is intensified by his encounter with the Ghost, who lays upon him the task of revenging 'his foul and most unnatural murder.' He swears to do so, and, driven close to madness by the enormity of the task, is reported to have confronted his girlfriend Ophelia with, she tells her father Polonius,

                        a sigh so piteous and profound
    That it did seem to shatter all his bulk
    And end his being.

                                          (2.1.95–7)

His state of mind mystifies both the court and Hamlet himself:

    I have of late—but wherefore I know not—lost all my mirth,
    forgone all custom of exercise; and indeed it goes so heavily with
    my disposition that this goodly frame, the earth, seems to me a
    sterile promontory (2.2.297–301)

he says to Rosencrantz and Guildenstern, whom the King and
Queen have summoned to spy upon him.

When a troupe of strolling players visit Elsinore Hamlet seeks to
test the truth of the Ghost's accusations by persuading them to
insert into the play they are performing for the court an episode
which he hopes will lead Claudius to reveal his guilt. And when
their leader vividly enacts a fictional grief Hamlet lashes himself
with words in the soliloquy beginning 'O what a rogue and
peasant slave am I', blaming himself for failing to take the
expression of his own, very real grief a step further, to the action
of revenge. But he cannot both obey the Ghost and remain true
to himself. For him to kill the King would—and will—be to bring
about his own death. And though he is attracted by death as a
relief from suffering, he fears it as 'an undiscovered country', as we
learn from his central meditation 'To be or not to be…', which
poses the idea of death as a great question mark, symbolized by
the Ghost and all his doubts about it.

Soon after this Hamlet himself, who has feigned madness, inflicts
death. His killing of Polonius is unplanned and accidental, almost
incidental, because when he stabs him behind the curtain in his
mother's room he is lost in obsessive disgust at her remarriage and
his desire to bring her to a state of penitent self-knowledge. His

47

attitudes are artfully designed to contrast with those of his victim's children. Polonius's daughter, Ophelia, retreats into genuine madness and finally will die a death that is not far from suicide. His son, Laertes, blazes into revengeful fury such as Hamlet might have expected himself to feel (though the analogy is not complete since Hamlet did not, like Laertes, know immediately and directly who had killed his father, or even that he had been murdered).

During the long period when Hamlet is absent from the stage—fictionally, in England—death and its effects continue to dominate the action, in the report of Ophelia's apparent suicide and with the plotting of the King and Laertes to kill Hamlet. And when Hamlet returns, it is to a graveyard in a scene (5.1) which mingles the play's most relaxed comedy with some of its most deeply reflective passages.

The scene is artfully structured. We have just heard Gertrude's account of Ophelia's drowning, so we know who is to be buried as we hear and see two workmen jokily discussing death in its most physical aspects. Death is the great leveller; the gravemaker alone makes houses that last till doomsday. Hamlet and Horatio come upon the scene, entering at first 'afar off', and Hamlet, knowing nothing of Ophelia's death, comments wryly on the discrepancy between the nature of the gravemaker's task and the way he carries it out. 'Hath this fellow no feeling of his business, that a sings at grave-making?'

In the scene's second stage the gravemaker throws up skulls, traditional emblems of mortality, which provoke Hamlet to reflect satirically on human vanity. The secret hidden from him comes a little closer as the gravedigger says he's digging the grave for neither man nor woman but for 'one that was a woman, sir, but, rest her soul, she's dead.' And he talks of Hamlet (who is overhearing him) who 'was mad and is sent into England', where his madness would not be noticed because 'there the men are as mad as he.'

When the gravedigger identifies one of the skulls as Yorick's we see Hamlet in the pose pictured earlier. He draws the moral that even the greatest of men will descend to this, and Shakespeare invokes the once mighty Julius Caesar:

> Imperial Caesar, dead and turned to clay,
> Might stop a hole to keep the wind away.
>
> (5.1.208–9)

Soon a funeral procession appears. We know it is Ophelia who is to be buried, but so far Hamlet does not; tension rises as first the Priest reveals that this is the body of a suicide, then Laertes that it is his sister and curses the very Hamlet who is watching him, leaping into the grave in a paroxysm of grief. He is behaving with the uninhibited emotional directness that Hamlet wishes he had been able to achieve on hearing of his father's death.

And now at last Hamlet too, leaping into the grave in a great theatrical gesture, is able to express himself in an affirmation at once of love, of personal identity, and of kingship:

> What is he whose grief
> Bears such an emphasis, whose phrase of sorrow
> Conjures the wand'ring stars and makes them stand
> Like wonder-wounded hearers? This is I,
> Hamlet the Dane.
>
> (5.1.250–4)

The scene has moved from the matter-of-fact attitudes to death of the gravediggers to a profound expression of the value of a single life and of the anguish that death can cause. After this Hamlet is able to tell Horatio that he will feel perfectly justified in killing Claudius and indeed that he has a moral duty to do so:

> —is't not perfect conscience
> To quit him with this arm? And is't not to be damned

> To let this canker of our nature come
> In further evil?
>
> (5.2.68–71)

It is a clear statement of belief on Hamlet's part, if not of Shakespeare's, in the morality of inflicting death in the hope of righting a wrong. Hamlet sees himself as a kind of surgeon to his country. He knows that the duel he will fight with Laertes is likely to bring about his own death, and he faces up to this with apparent stoicism:

> There's a special providence in the fall of a sparrow. If it be now, 'tis not to come. If it be not to come, it will be now. If it be not now, yet it will come. The readiness is all. (5.2.165–8)

Finally he reaches a state in which, having learned that he has been fatally wounded by Laertes' sword which was poisoned by the King's command, he can kill the King with no scruples, so avenging not only his father's death but also his mother's and the act that will bring about his own. He dies with courtly grace, displaying a touch of humour as he speaks of death as a policeman, the 'fell sergeant' who is 'strict in his arrest', before he subsides into silence.

Tracing a single theme through the play, as I have tried to do, does less than justice to the abundant richness of this extraordinary text, which represents a great leap forward in Shakespeare's creativity. *Hamlet* includes many elements of Elizabethan popular theatre: a ghost, a sententious father figure (Polonius), a play within the play, dumb shows, topical satire, sudden death, a chase, a musical mad scene, a comedy routine for 'clowns', a duel, and a final holocaust of deaths. And tragic though the main plot is, Shakespeare constantly maintains a comic perspective on the action, through irony, satire, and sarcasm. There is no wonder that the neo-classical French critic Voltaire was so shocked by the play's defiance of all the rules of tragedy that he wrote of it as:

a coarse and barbarous piece, which would not be tolerated by the
lowest rabble of France and Italy. In it Hamlet becomes mad in the
second act, his mistress becomes mad in the third; the prince kills
the father of his mistress under pretence of killing a rat, and the
heroine throws herself into the river. A grave is dug upon the stage,
the grave-diggers indulge in quibbles worthy of themselves, while
holding in their hands the skulls of the dead. Prince Hamlet
responds to their abominable vulgarities by stuff no less disgusting.
In the meanwhile another of the actors conquers Poland.

*Hamlet* is a baroque masterpiece, not a neatly constructed play
like, for instance, *The Comedy of Errors*, or *Romeo and Juliet*, or
*Julius Caesar*. Here Shakespeare's imagination 'o'erflows the
measure' (to quote a phrase from *Antony and Cleopatra*, which is
no less prodigal in invention). In current stage practice it usually
loses 800 or so lines, and Shakespeare himself is unlikely to have
expected that every word he wrote would have been performed at
one go. Some passages, such as the topical satire on boys' acting
companies (2.2.339–63), Hamlet's advice to the players and their
play (3.2), Hamlet's satire on lawyers in the graveyard, and the
affectations of the foppish Osric (5.2.112–30) are easily shortened
or omitted.

In this play Shakespeare's techniques of characterization through
language in both verse and prose, previously most brilliantly
displayed in *Romeo and Juliet*, are deployed with easy mastery.
They are apparent in the awesomely sonorous utterances of the
Ghost; in the glibness with which Claudius addresses Hamlet in
the first court scene; in the sententiousness with which Polonius
speaks to Laertes; in the fragmentary utterances of the mad
Ophelia; the earthy rusticities of the gravedigger and his mate;
and the linguistic affectedness of the foppish Osric. And they are
apparent above all in the extraordinary range of both verse and
prose spoken by Hamlet himself. The character of Hamlet is so
sensitive, so volatile, so responsive to every wind that blows that he
might almost be said to have no character, or at least to have a

character that is in constant flux, in search of its own identity until, perhaps, the closing scenes of the play when, having outfaced Laertes over Ophelia's corpse, he reaches a kind of equilibrium.

In the first court scene, Claudius rebukes Hamlet for excessive mourning with oily eloquence which sounds scripted:

> to persever
> In obstinate condolement is a course
> Of impious stubbornness, 'tis unmanly grief,
> It shows a will most incorrect to heaven,
> A heart unfortified, a mind impatient,
> An understanding simple and unschooled;
> ...      Fie, 'tis a fault to heaven,
> A fault against the dead, a fault to nature,
> To reason most absurd, whose common theme
> Is death of fathers, and who still hath cried
> From the first corpse till he that died today,
> 'This must be so'.
>
> (1.2.92–7, 1.2.101–6)

The immediacy with which Hamlet speaks when he is left alone seems to allow us access to the very processes of his mind. The closest that Shakespeare had previously come to this style of writing is in Juliet's Nurse's account of her charge's childhood (1.3.18–59), but Hamlet's stream-of-consciousness mode of utterance betokens high intelligence, a racing intellect that can scarcely keep up with itself, rather than absence of mental discipline:

> Heaven and earth,
> Must I remember? Why, she would hang on him
> As if increase of appetite had grown
> By what it fed on, and yet within a month—
> Let me not think on't; frailty, thy name is woman—
> A little month, or ere those shoes were old
> With which she followed my poor father's body,

>     Like Niobe, all tears, why she, even she—
>     O God, a beast that wants discourse of reason
>     Would have mourned longer!—married with mine uncle...
>                                   (1.2.142–51)

*Hamlet* enjoyed exceptional popularity in Shakespeare's own
time, especially among what one early commentator called 'the
wiser sort', and it remained popular in a shortened but not
seriously adapted version on the London stage when theatres
reopened in the 1640s after the Puritan closure.

In the 18th century David Garrick made a great hit in the title part,
but towards the end of his career, responding to neo-classical
objections of the kind made by Voltaire, he drastically altered what
he called 'all the rubbish of the fifth act', going so far as to eliminate
the gravediggers. But towards the end of the 18th century, with the
dawning of the Age of Sensibility and the Romantic period, the
original play (almost always abbreviated, often very heavily)
came into its own in England and, gradually, overseas. Goethe's
discussion in his novel *Wilhelm Meister* of 1795 portrayed a
willowy figure whose high sensibility made him unequal to the
burden of revenge placed upon him, and since then the play and its
central character have been subject to such a wide range of
interpretations that in 1874 the satirist W. S. Gilbert, in a short
comic play called *Rosencrantz and Guildenstern*, caused Ophelia to
say, in response to the question of whether Hamlet was mad,

>             Some men hold
>     That he's the sanest, far, of all sane men—
>     Some that he's really sane, but shamming mad—
>     Some that he's really mad, but shamming sane—
>     Some that he will be mad, some that he was,
>     Some that he couldn't be. But on the whole—
>     —As far as I can make out what they mean—
>     The favourite theory's somewhat like this:
>     Hamlet is idiotically sane
>     With lucid intervals of lunacy.

In many 20th-century productions and later, Hamlet has been seen as an archetypal rebel against society, and the play, often in translation and in more or less heavily adapted form, has been used as a political platform for many different causes. The director Peter Hall said of it in 1965: 'It turns a new face to each century, even to each decade. It is a mirror which gives back the reflection of the age that is contemplating it.' It is one of the most malleable of texts, a constant stimulus to thought, and an unfailing source of theatrical pleasure.

# Chapter 6
## *Othello*

Like *Romeo and Juliet*, *Othello* is a fictional love tragedy focusing on two private individuals whose lives, unlike those of figures such as Titus, Hamlet, and Macbeth, are not bound up with the fate of nations. Also like *Romeo and Juliet*, the play is based on an Italian tale, this time a prosaic story of love and jealousy by Giraldi Cinthio which Shakespeare romanticizes and dignifies. But here the principal focus is not on both lovers equally—as it will be in *Antony and Cleopatra*—but on the man, and the tragedy is the outcome not of the operations of a malignant fate but of the personal vendetta waged against the Moorish general Othello, operating in the service of Venice, by his subordinate, the ensign Iago; and the woman, Othello's wife, Desdemona, is the tragic victim, not an equal partner (Figure 5).

Compact, fast-moving, tensely dramatic, emotionally compelling, and rising to a riveting tragic conclusion with the murder of Desdemona by Othello followed by his suicide, this is an immensely effective piece of theatre written in dialogue, sometimes racy and conversational, which rises to great heights of eloquence. Popular in its time, *Othello* was one of the first of Shakespeare's plays to be revived after the Restoration of the monarchy in 1660, and survived a critical attack of 1693 by Thomas Rymer which forms a salutary lesson in the dangers of

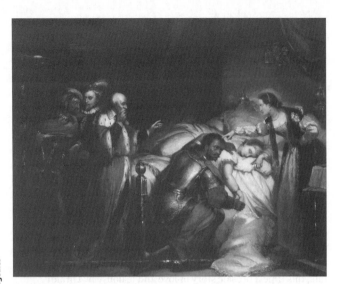

5. **The Death of Desdemona, *c.*1857. William Slater, oil painting.**

applying inappropriate criteria to works of art; he caustically described it as 'a bloody farce' and as 'a caution to all maidens of quality how, without their parents' consent, they run away with blackamoors.' Alluding to the part played in the plot by Desdemona's loss of her handkerchief he describes the play reductively as 'a warning to all good wives that they look well to their linen.' His racist comment that 'with us a Moor might marry some little drab or small-coal wench' foreshadows later objections to the propriety of portraying a black man as a tragic hero. And his shocked description of the play as a 'bloody farce', deriving from the neo-classical view that comic elements are inappropriate to tragedy, reflects total misunderstanding of Shakespeare's attitude to the different kinds of drama. There are indeed strong comic elements in the play, and for sympathetic audiences they both enhance its theatrical appeal and broaden its emotional range.

More than any other of Shakespeare's plays except *The Taming of the Shrew*, *Othello* represents a battle of wits between its two central characters, the rationalist Iago, who often speaks in prose, and the romantic Othello, whose natural medium is verse, but who lapses first into prose, and then into incoherent gibberish under Iago's corrupting influence. Desdemona and Iago's wife, Emilia, are the innocent victims destroyed between them.

Racial issues have always been important to the play's story of personal conflict. Its full title as it was first printed (in 1622, some twenty years after it was written)—*The Tragedy of Othello, the Moor of Venice*—tells us that this is the tragic story of a black man, an outsider in an exotically foreign society. 'Tragedy' would have come as a surprise; the word implies at least a degree of sympathy, and playgoers of the time were not accustomed to being invited to sympathize with black people; Aaron the Moor, in *Titus Andronicus*, who declares 'If one good deed in all my life I did / I do repent it from my very soul' (5.3.188–9), is far more typical. Devils in ecclesiastical wall paintings were represented as black, and Othello recalls such paintings when, after hearing that Desdemona has denied that he killed her, he poignantly says, in an agony of remorse, 'She's like a liar gone to burning hell', to which her maid, Emilia, responds with 'the more angel she, and you the blacker devil!' (5.2.138–40).

Shakespeare capitalizes heavily on issues of colour, and his first audiences, seeing the actor Richard Burbage in black make-up, might well have been predisposed to believe the contemptuous terms in which Iago speaks of Othello in the opening scene, with their imputations of sexual licence: 'an old black ram', 'a Barbary horse', 'a lascivious Moor'. Characters within the play refer disparagingly to Othello's race: Iago calls him 'thick-lips', Brabanzio—Desdemona's father—speaks of his 'sooty bosom', and Othello himself, after Iago's accusations against Desdemona, fears that 'My name, that was as fresh / As Dian's visage, is now begrimed and black / As mine own face' (3.3.391–3).

Later ages have shared some of the racial prejudices voiced by Thomas Rymer, and have allowed them to influence performance. Charles Lamb found that anyone seeing the play acted must 'find something extremely revolting in the courtship and wedded caresses of Othello and Desdemona.' The poet Coleridge thought it 'would be something monstrous to conceive the beautiful Venetian girl falling in love with a veritable negro'; and when the first black actor to play the role, Ira Aldridge, who had been virtually banished from his native America because of his colour, acted (successfully) at Covent Garden, in 1832, he was nevertheless vilified in the press as a 'miserable nigger', a 'wretched upstart' who was 'about to defile the stage.' The great black singing actor Paul Robeson, too, when playing the role in London in 1930, faced opposition on racial grounds.

In more recent times the wheel has come full circle to such an extent that well-qualified white actors have been denied the opportunity to play the role. This is understandable in social terms but runs the risk of undermining the self-conscious symbolism of Shakespeare's play. Bianca, the name of Cassio's mistress, means 'white', and Shakespeare frequently plays on paradoxes that associate outer with inner qualities, blackness of skin with inner evil in a way that may be more effective if the audience know that the actor is not really black. 'I saw Othello's visage in his mind', says Desdemona, defending her choice of husband, and the Duke of Venice supports her, saying to her aggrieved father:

> And, noble signor,
> If virtue no delighted beauty lack,
> Your son-in-law is far more fair than black.
> (1.3.288–90)

The malice and evil-spiritedness of Iago are firmly established in his opening dialogue with Desdemona's foolish suitor Roderigo, to whom he freely admits that he follows Othello, whom he hates 'as I do hell pains', only 'to serve my turn upon him', feigning 'love and duty...for my peculiar end.' And we rapidly learn that Iago's hatred for Othello centres on the fact that Othello has chosen Cassio, not Iago, as his lieutenant.

Roderigo joins in Iago's racial and sexual vilification of Othello, saying that Desdemona has eloped with 'a lascivious Moor', but as soon as Othello appears Shakespeare works to overturn whatever prejudice the audience may have felt against his black hero, who responds with calm dignity to Brabanzio's accusations that he can have won Desdemona only by practising black magic. And when Brabanzio repeats his accusations before the Duke of Venice and the full Senate, Shakespeare gives Othello a calm and dignified speech of self-defence:

> That I have ta'en away this old man's daughter,
> It is most true, true I have married her.
> The very head and front of my offending
> Hath this extent, no more.
>
> (1.3.78–81)

He speaks of how, in his wooing, he told Desdemona about his romantic, heroic past:

> Of moving accidents by flood and field,
> Of hair-breadth scapes i'th'imminent deadly breach,
> Of being taken by the insolent foe
> And sold to slavery...
>
> (1.3.134–7)

And he says he told her about:

> the cannibals that each other eat,
> The Anthropophagi, and men whose heads
> Do grow beneath their shoulders.
>
> (1.3.142–4)

Was he kidding her with these travellers' tales? Or does he really think he has seen these things? His tales of wonder may give us an early intimation of the credulity that will be his downfall, that will make him attach such superstitious importance to the handkerchief, his first gift to Desdemona, with 'magic in the web of it', which Iago will make him believe Desdemona has thoughtlessly given to Cassio, and which becomes a symbol of the way his love for her can be blown away by Iago's lies and machinations.

> Trifles light as air
> Are to the jealous confirmations strong
> As proofs of holy writ.
>
> (3.3.326–8)

Iago's hatred of Othello is notoriously vague and various in motivation. Coleridge famously referred to his 'motiveless malignity', but in fact he offers a variety of reasons for it besides his jealousy of Roderigo's promotion. He says he loves Desdemona himself (2.1.90) and that he suspects Othello of adultery with his own wife, Emilia; but there is a purity about his evil which adds to his fascination as a dramatic character, as if Shakespeare were suggesting that it is futile to look for normal causes of an abnormal state of mind. He is a psychopath, and a consummate actor, 'honest' Iago to everyone in the play (including Othello) until the final revelation of his villainy.

In Iago, Shakespeare offers a devastating revelation of the limitations of reasonableness. Like Edmond in *King Lear*, Iago can use reason, can be as we say 'reasonable', to deceive people who are much wiser than he. Love is meaningless to him. He reduces it to mere sexuality, telling Roderigo that it is 'merely a lust of the blood and a permission of the will', that when Desdemona 'is sated' with Othello's body she will be ready for a younger lover. Othello's 'free and open nature' makes him 'think men honest that but seem to be so'; Iago is 'honest' to all the world except to us, the audience. In soliloquy he drops the mask.

> The Moor is of a free and open nature,
> That thinks men honest that but seem to be so,
> And will as tenderly be led by th' nose
> As asses are.
>
> (1.3.391–4)

And within a moment his plot is hatched.

> I ha't. It is ingendered. Hell and night
> Must bring this monstrous birth to the world's light.
>
> (1.3.395–6)

Iago's confidentiality with the audience means that we have a frightening sense of complicity with him, as if we could all too easily act as he does. As he leads Othello by the nose, he takes us much of the way with him, vertiginously in danger of losing our moral bearings in admiration of the virtuosity with which he manipulates Othello's emotions. The great 'temptation scene' (3.3) in which Othello is transformed from a sensible man into a beast is heralded by Iago's statement of intent:

> whiles this honest fool [Cassio]
> Plies Desdemona to repair his fortune,
> And she for him pleads strongly to the Moor,
> I'll pour this pestilence into his ear:
> That she repeals him for her body's lust,
> And by how much she strives to do him good
> She shall undo her credit with the Moor.
>
> (2.3.344–50)

Shakespeare is not trying to keep us in suspense: we know what is likely to happen, and our pleasure as theatregoers will be to watch it unfold before us. This is a kind of seduction scene. Detaching Othello's affections from Desdemona, Iago attaches them to himself, so that part way through the process Othello can say, chillingly, 'I am bound to thee for ever' (3.3.217), and the scene ends, after the pair have knelt together in a ghastly parody of religious ritual in which Othello swears revenge and Iago dedicates himself to his service, with 'I am your own for ever.'

The breaking of the bonds of love shakes the very foundations of Othello's being, eliciting from him speeches of anguished eloquence as he takes farewell of the life he had known:

> Farewell the tranquil mind, farewell content,
> Farewell the plumèd troops and the big wars
> That makes ambition virtue!
>
> (3.3.353–5)

From this he descends to the gibberish of 'Pish! Noses, ears and lips! Is't possible? Confess? Handkerchief? O devil!', and physically from the upright posture of the dignified commander to the ignominious falling down into a fit in which Iago can exult over him. Early in the scene he had said of Desdemona:

> Perdition catch my soul
> But I do love thee, and when I love thee not,
> Chaos has come again.
>
> (3.3.91–3).

Now it has, and it does.

The play has only three female characters, and they are easily graded on the moral scale. Bianca has a clearly erotic relationship with Cassio, and Iago despises her as 'A hussy that by selling her desires / Buys herself bread and cloth', implying that she is no better than a prostitute. Emilia, the respectably married wife, also despises Bianca as a strumpet. This doesn't seem easily compatible with Iago's statement that Cassio has 'a daily beauty in his life', but she is certainly the least virtuous woman in the play.

Emilia occupies a higher place on the morality scale, but she is no angel either. The play has a touchingly meditative episode (4.3) in which Desdemona sings the 'song of willow' that will not go from her mind as Emilia helps her to prepare for bed after the terrible scene in which Othello, believing in her guilt, has treated her like a whore in a brothel. The 'poor soul' in the song has 'called [her lover] false love', to which the lover has retorted cynically 'If I court more women, you'll couch with more men.' Desdemona can't believe that women should 'abuse their husbands / In such gross kind'; she herself would not do so 'for all the world', but Emilia takes a more down-to-earth attitude:

> Marry, I would not do such a thing for a joint ring, nor for measures
> of lawn, nor for gowns, petticoats, nor caps nor any petty exhibition;
> but for all the whole world? Ud's pity, who would not make her
> husband a cuckold to make him a monarch? I should venture
> purgatory for't.  (4.3.71–6)

When Desdemona still refuses to believe she would do such a thing, Emilia launches into a vehement claim that women should have equal sexual rights with men in a speech that seems far ahead of its time. It is 'their husbands' faults', she says 'If wives do fall.' If men fail in their marital duties:

> And pour our treasures into foreign laps,
> Or else break out in peevish jealousies,
> Throwing restraint upon us; or say they strike us,
> Or scant our former having in despite:
> Why, we have galls; and though we have some grace,
> Yet have we some revenge.
>
> (4.3.87–92)

Women have 'affections, desires for sport, and frailty, as men have', and if men are tempted to stray, they can only expect their wives to do so, too. But Desdemona remains adamant that she would

63

not follow bad example. Shakespeare leaves us in no doubt of her moral integrity. And though Emilia expresses less idealistic principles than her mistress, she rises to moral greatness in the final scene, with her passionate defence of Desdemona, her denunciation of Iago, and her determination to die by her mistress's side.

After Othello has recovered from the fit induced by Iago's taunting, he sees himself as a man transformed into a beast: 'A hornèd man' (that is, a man who wears the horns traditionally associated with cuckoldry) is 'a monster and a beast' (4.1.60). Certainly his behaviour under Iago's influence, culminating in his smothering of Desdemona, is monstrous and beastly. But, convinced that his cause is just, he recovers his dignity of speech, grieving over the outward beauty of Desdemona's white skin, 'smooth as monumental alabaster', intoxicated by her 'balmy breath, that doth almost persuade / Justice to break her sword!', seeing his intention to kill her as 'a sacrifice', not a murder. Having smothered her, he expresses horror at his deed even before he knows that Desdemona is innocent:

> O insupportable, O heavy hour!
> Methinks it should be now a huge eclipse
> Of sun and moon, and that th'affrighted globe
> Should yawn at alteration.
>
> (5.2.107–10)

And his intense anguish when he knows that Iago has deceived him affords him an awesome vision of purgatorial suffering like those represented in ecclesiastical depictions of hell:

> Whip me, ye devils,
> From the possession of this heavenly sight,
> Blow me about in winds, roast me in sulphur,
> Wash me in steep-down gulfs of liquid fire!
>
> (5.2.284–7)

In his last big speech he recovers the authority with which he had addressed the Venetian senators early in the action. He asks to be remembered as:

> ...one that loved not wisely, but too well,
> ...one not easily jealous but, being wrought,
> Perplexed in the extreme;

> (5.2.353–5)

But it is also a speech of self-condemnation, and it culminates, as he reveals a concealed weapon, in an intensely theatrical act of self-execution.

Does this redeem him? Not everyone thinks so. He has been accused of being self-deluded and self-dramatizing in the closing moments of the play. But Cassio pays tribute to him: 'he was great of heart.' And all join in condemnation of Iago who, sentenced to torture, remains implacably silent as he looks 'on the tragic loading of this bed.'

Although shifting attitudes to race have played a significant part in the history of the play's reception and in the ways it has been staged, it has both held its place in the theatrical repertoire and generated numerous offshoots—an opera by Rossini and Verdi's late masterpiece *Otello*, ballets, orchestral music, and films, some deriving from theatrical productions, such as those starring Laurence Olivier (1965) and Trevor Nunn's production of 1989 given in the Royal Shakespeare Company's studio theatre, The Other Place, with Willard White as Othello and Ian McKellen as Iago, as well as studio-based films such as that starring Orson Welles (1952) and the one (1995) with Laurence Fishburne as Othello and Kenneth Branagh as Iago. The play's focus on human beings in a social setting means that it can easily be updated: the setting of the Nunn production recalls mid-19th-century America, and a National Theatre version of 2011, with Rory Kinnear as Iago and Adrian Lester as Othello, set the bulk of the action in a present-day military camp. There is even a rock *Othello, Catch my Soul* (1968).

# Chapter 7
## *Macbeth*

> pity, like a naked newborn babe,
> Striding the blast, or heaven's cherubim, horsed
> Upon the sightless couriers of the air,
> Shall blow the horrid deed in every eye
> That tears shall drown the wind.
>
> (*Macbeth*, 1.7, 21–5; Figure 6)

'*Thunder and lightning. Enter three Witches*'. We are on a blasted heath somewhere in Scotland—or is it only in our own imaginations? And the witches (we later learn)—are 'withered', and 'wild in their attire'; and they commune with familiar spirits called Paddock and Grimalkin; and they look like women but have beards; and a battle is about to take place; and the witches expect soon to meet someone called Macbeth; and they speak—or chant—of topsy-turvydom—'Fair is foul, and foul is fair'; and within seconds they vanish, three wicked shudders, in another crack of thunder and flash of lightning, as quickly as they appeared.

It's clear from the start that this is going to be no chronicle of the daily lives of ordinary people. And as it goes on we see someone addressing a dagger that is not really there; and a woman calling on spirits to unsex her; and we hear about horses eating each other; and see a ghost appear—twice—at a state banquet; and the witches again dancing around a cauldron into which they

**6. 'pity, like a naked new-born babe'. William Blake's print, *c*.1795.**

throw an assortment of horrific objects, and singing 'Double, double, toil and trouble, / Fire burn, and cauldron bubble', and calling up weird apparitions, and a 'show of eight kings'; and actors pretending to be an army pretending to be a forest; and finally the imitation head of a king on the end of a spear.

It is not only in its use of the supernatural, and of conventions associated with the contemporary theatre such as people speaking in verse, soliloquies, asides, witches, ghosts, a dumb show, and a severed head that *Macbeth* is very much of its time. When it was first seen, around 1606, its subject matter was highly topical. King James I, the patron of the acting company that performed it—the King's Men—was also King James VI of Scotland and had been on the English throne only since 1603. He had a strong personal interest in witchcraft, both as the author of a book—*Demonology*, published in 1597 and reprinted in 1603—demonstrating his belief in it and because he had been the intended victim of people who believed themselves to have supernatural powers as well as having taken part in trials that had resulted in the execution of a number of supposed witches, some of whom had later—too late to do them any good—been declared innocent.

Moreover a play about the murder of a Scottish king (Duncan) was peculiarly topical in the aftermath of the Gunpowder Plot of 1605, designed to blow up not just King James along with members of his family but the entire English parliament, which is obliquely referred to in the Porter's reference to equivocation—the technique used by secret Roman Catholics of appearing to say one thing while meaning another.

Even more directly, Macbeth actually refers to the line of King James when he speaks of kings 'That twofold balls and treble sceptres carry'—an allusion to James's unification of the kingdoms of England and Scotland—in the show of eight kings that the witches conjure up before him (4.1.128–40), an episode that would have had very special significance when the play was performed at court, before the King himself. (It is usually omitted in modern performance.) *Macbeth* is the most obviously topical—and to that extent dated—of Shakespeare's plays both in its dramaturgy and in its subject matter.

The play was first printed in the Folio of 1623, and is the shortest of Shakespeare's tragedies. The text that has come down to us is believed to be an adaptation by Thomas Middleton—co-author with Shakespeare of *Timon of Athens*—of the orginal play which he may have shortened and to which he added the episodes in which Hecate, goddess of witchcraft and the night, appears to the witches, and which call for the performance of two songs also found in Middleton's play *The Witch*. In the Folio these songs are identified only by their opening lines, but the Oxford *Complete Works* of 1986 prints them in full.

In spite of being very much of its own time—perhaps more so than any other Shakespeare play—*Macbeth* has been and remains popular on stage and on film, both as it was originally printed and in adaptation, and is often studied in schools and in universities. Even young children can enjoy the fanciful weirdness of the witches. The play exerts an imaginative appeal that transcends topicality. With our rational minds we may deny its basic premises, rejecting the notion that people could ever have behaved like this, yet it works on our imaginations on a subconscious level, appealing to our sense that, as Hamlet puts it in a play that also draws on the supernatural, 'there are more things in heaven and earth than are dreamt of' in our philosophy; that perhaps after all some people do have the gift of seeing into the future, and can return from the grave; and that, as Macbeth puts it, 'Stones have been known to move, and trees to speak' (3.4.121–2).

The basic story of the play, which Shakespeare found in Holinshed's *Chronicles*, one of his favourite source books, could provide the basis for a crude melodrama, entirely lacking in human reality. What gives the play its greatness is the psychological reality with which Shakespeare invests his central characters through the power of his writing and the depths of his imaginative identification with their innermost beings. As in a great painting by Rembrandt, roles of secondary importance are drained of individuality, throwing all the emphasis on the central characters. Duncan, for instance, is a symbol rather than a portrait of an ideal king. Banquo is important mainly because, though he is subject to the same temptations as Macbeth, he resists them. He tells Macbeth that he has dreamed of the witches:

> I dreamt last night of the weird sisters.
> To you they have showed some truth.

Macbeth replies in lines that suggest uncertainty of how far he can go with Banquo:

69

> I think not of them;
> Yet, when we can entreat an hour to serve,
> We would spend it in some words upon that business
> If you would grace the time.

Banquo agrees, and Macbeth is encouraged to go further:

> If you shall cleave to my consent when 'tis,
> It shall make honour for you.

But now Banquo withdraws:

> So I lose none
> In seeking to augment it, but still keep
> My bosom franchised and allegiance clear,
> I shall be counselled.
>
> (2.1.19–28)

This is dialogue of psychological nuance, in which Banquo expresses both to Macbeth and to us his imperviousness to temptation without actually having been tempted. He becomes a kind of embodied conscience to Macbeth.

The stylization evident in Shakespeare's portrayal of lesser characters throws into relief the subtlety and psychological penetration with which he takes us into the inner beings of Macbeth and his wife. The evil within both of them constantly finds expression in a suppression of natural feeling. In a great invocation Lady Macbeth makes a fiercely conscious effort to suppress her womanhood:

> Come, you spirits
> That tend on mortal thoughts, unsex me here,
> And fill me from the crown to the toe top-full
> Of direst cruelty. Make thick my blood,
> Stop up th'access and passage to remorse,

That no compunctious visitings of nature
Shake my fell purpose, nor keep peace between
Th'effect and it. Come to my woman's breasts,
And take my milk for gall, you murd'ring ministers,
Wherever in your sightless substances
You wait on nature's mischief. Come, thick night,
And pall thee in the dunnest smoke of hell,
That my keen knife see not the wound it makes
Nor heaven peep through the blanket of the dark
To cry 'Hold, hold!'

(1.5.39–53)

Macbeth, on the other hand, allows his imagination full rein in a manner that almost overcomes his evil ambitions:

this Duncan
Hath borne his faculties so meek, hath been
So clear in his great office, that his virtues
Will plead like angels, trumpet-tongued against
The deep damnation of his taking-off;
And pity, like a naked newborn babe,
Striding the blast, or heaven's cherubim, horsed
Upon the sightless couriers of the air,
Shall blow the horrid deed in every eye
That tears shall drown the wind. I have no spur
To prick the sides of my intent, but only
Vaulting ambition which o'erleaps itself
And falls on th' other.

(1.7.16–28)

Before the murder there is a clear contrast between Macbeth and Lady Macbeth. But as the action progresses their roles are reversed. Lady Macbeth's imagination begins to work. Both of them, who had called upon night to cover their deeds, find that Macbeth 'hath murdered sleep' (2.2.40). They have terrible dreams. They had turned day into night, but now their nights are indistinguishable from day. She had hoped to 'make trifles of terrors' (*All's Well That Ends Well*, 2.3.2) when she should have submitted herself to fear of the unknown; but when her imagination begins to kick in, her 'seeming knowledge' gives way to the horrified questions of the sleep-walking scene which shows, with an extraordinary anticipation of the theories of Freudian psychology, the release in sleep of the subconscious fears that she has suppressed in her waking life. She had thought that 'a little water clears us of this deed'; now she finds that 'all the perfumes of Arabia will not sweeten this little hand.'

In Macbeth, by contrast, we witness a slow death of the imagination. He had been so horrified when he imagined the consequences of the murder he was contemplating that he almost abandoned the plan. Sheer impetus of accumulated evil has thrust him into a career of escalating crime.

> I am in blood
> Stepped in so far that, should I wade no more,
> Returning were as tedious as go o'er.
>
> (3.4.135–7)

From murdering Duncan himself he has descended to having Banquo assassinated by professional murderers, and from that to bringing about the slaughter of Lady Macduff and her son—murder of a child being symbolically the ultimate crime—by remote control, like a politician pressing a button to release distant nuclear forces. His worst crimes are committed with none of that awareness of evil that he had felt in contemplating the murder of Duncan.

> The castle of Macduff I will surprise,
> Seize upon Fife, give to th'edge o'th'sword
> His wife, his babes, and all unfortunate souls
> That trace him in his line.
>
> (4.1.166–9)

At least he acknowledges that they are 'unfortunate'. He expresses an inner vision of despair:

> I have lived long enough. My way of life
> Is fall'n into the sere, the yellow leaf,
> And that which should accompany old age,
> As honour, love, obedience, troops of friends,
> I must not look to have, but in their stead,
> Curses, not loud but deep, mouth-honour, breath
> Which the poor heart would fain deny and dare not.
>
> (5.3.24–30)

His responses are numbed: 'I have almost forgot the taste of fears'. And when he hears of his wife's death his reaction is not so much an expression of personal grief as a denial of the validity of all human emotion:

> She should have died hereafter.
> There would have been a time for such a word.
> Tomorrow, and tomorrow, and tomorrow
> Creeps in this petty pace from day to day
> To the last syllable of recorded time,
> And all our yesterdays have lighted fools
> The way to dusty death. Out, out, brief candle.
> Life's but a walking shadow, a poor player
> That struts and frets his hour upon the stage,
> And then is heard no more. It is a tale
> Told by an idiot, full of sound and fury,
> Signifying nothing.
>
> (5.5.16–27)

Although *Macbeth* is a historical tragedy, it is also a kind of parable that can easily be related to very different areas of human life. Ambitious men who quell scruples of conscience to fulfil their ambitions, and who are helped to do so by no less ambitious partners, are found in all societies at all times, so it is easy to reimagine the basic story in different times and societies. There are fine film and video versions, such as those starring Orson Welles (1948), Polanski's film of 1971, the 1976 studio production directed by Trevor Nunn starring Ian McKellen and Judi Dench, Gregory Doran's Royal Shakespeare Company version of 2001, starring Antony Sher and Harriet Walter, and that starring Michael Fassbender (2015), which stay reasonably close to the original text and setting; but there are also more radically adapted versions, such as the film *Joe Macbeth* (1955), which relates the action to gang warfare in Chicago, the outstanding Japanese film, *Throne of Blood*, directed by Akiro Kurosawa (1957 ), and the Indian *Maqbool* (2004), set in the Mumbai underworld, which demonstrate that the play can transcend its initial topicality to be seen as an enduring projection of basic human instincts and desires.

# Chapter 8
## *King Lear*

*King Lear* is the Mount Everest of plays. For many actors, the journey to its summit represents the high point of their careers (though you don't have to be old to succeed in the role: Paul Scofield was only 40 when he played it in one of the most highly admired of productions, by Peter Brook in 1962). A complication for the reader is that the play exists in two different versions, one printed in the Oxford *Complete Works* as *The History of King Lear* and based on the play as Shakespeare first wrote it, the other, apparently a later theatrical adaptation, as *The Tragedy of King Lear*. Theatre directors usually pick and choose between the two, and often shorten the play anyway. To avoid unnecessary complications, I shall concentrate on the later version.

For readers as well as for performers the play may seem a daunting intellectual and emotional challenge. William Hazlitt, in an eloquent essay of 1817, called it 'the best of all Shakespeare's plays, for it is the one in which he was the most in earnest'—not perhaps the most inviting of recommendations. And the 18th-century editor and critic Samuel Johnson, while writing that 'There is perhaps no play which keeps the attention so strongly fixed; which so much agitates our passions and interests our curiosity', nevertheless also wrote that he 'was many years ago so shocked by Cordelia's death, that I know not whether I ever endured to read again the last scenes of the play till I undertook to revise them as an editor.'

Of course, the play tells a deeply tragic story, a story of national and familial division and paternal oppression; of hypocritical deception; of developing enmity between sisters (Goneril and Regan) and between brothers (Edmond and Edgar); of profound physical cruelty climaxing in an onstage episode in which one man (the Earl of Cornwall), abetted by his wife, deliberately and cold-bloodedly blinds another (the Earl of Gloucester). It culminates in Gloucester's attempted suicide, in a fight to the death between brothers (Edgar and Edmond again); in the poisoning of one sister (Goneril) by another (Regan); and in the slaughter offstage of a young woman (Cordelia) whose father (King Lear) carries her body on stage and exhibits it to onlookers before himself expiring over it.

The story of the play—related to that of Cinderella and her two ugly sisters—has something of the nature of a parable, in which characters divide easily into the good, such as Edgar, Cordelia, the Earl of Kent, and Lear's Fool; the bad, such as Goneril, Regan, and (until the very end of his life) Edmond; and those of a middle sort, such as Lear himself, the Earl of Gloucester, and the Duke of Albany, whose attitude to the life around them changes in the course of the action. But this is also a profoundly human story in which a faithful attendant lord (the Earl of Kent) disguises himself so that he can serve his king (Lear) anonymously; another member of the royal household (the Fool) desperately tries to relieve his master's mental woes; a son (Edgar) disguises himself and voluntarily undergoes physical torment so that he can help to redeem his father (Gloucester); a loyal anonymous servant sacrifices his life on his master's (Gloucester's) behalf; a daughter (Cordelia) leads an army on her father's behalf and helps to bring him back from madness to sanity; and in which a divided kingdom is at last reunited even though only after terrible turmoil.

Shakespeare's Tragedies

76

And profoundly serious though the play is, it is shot through with comedy—though admittedly it's often a grotesque, ironic sort of comedy. We see it in Goneril and Regan's blatant hypocrisy in the opening scene; the Fool's wry attempts to teach Lear though parable and snatches of song; the Earl of Kent's brusque treatment of Goneril's servant Oswald; the rivalry of Goneril and Regan for Edmond's sexual favours; the mad Lear's mock-trial of Goneril; the bizarre, black comedy of Gloucester's attempted suicide; and the touching camaraderie of the mad Lear and the blinded Gloucester in the scene at Dover.

*King Lear* is the only one of Shakespeare's tragedies in which he interweaves one plot, centring on Lear, with another, centring on Gloucester, which is no less relevant to the play's overall effect. There is a clearly symbolic relationship between the two men. King Lear undergoes a purgatorial process of suffering which, though it involves bodily pain as he is lashed by the storm of wind and rain (Figure 7) into which his two elder daughters' cruelty impels him, is primarily a suffering of the mind. 'This tempest in my mind', he says, 'Doth from my senses take all feeling else / Save what beats there: filial ingratitude.' The Earl of Gloucester, on the other hand, undergoes the physical torment of being thrust out of his own home by his guests, and of having both his eyes plucked out in a horrific on-stage episode that has been known to cause strong men to faint. This parallelism of mind and body demonstrates the comprehensive scope of Shakespeare's ambition in this deeply human but totally unsentimental study of man in relation to the physical universe.

The story of King Lear, who was supposed to have lived in the 8th century BC and to have founded the city of Leicester (Leir-castrum), had often been told as part of the legendary history of Britain. Shakespeare could have read it in a number of books and certainly knew a tragi-comedy based on it which had been successfully acted in 1594 by a company—the Queen's Men—which may at one time have included the young Shakespeare himself. This play

7. The mad Lear in the storm (3.4), vividly suggesting the scene's mixture of the pathetic with the grotesque. The Fool, Edgar (wrapped in a blanket); Kent; Lear; Gloucester (with a torch). George Romney (1734–1802); oil painting.

reached print in 1605 under the title of *The moste famous Chronicle historye of Leire king of England and his Three Daughters*, shortly before Shakespeare wrote his play. In this version the story is heavily Christianized.

Shakespeare's total elimination of a Christian framework to the action provides the clearest possible indication of his desire to use the story as the basis for a fundamental examination of the human condition, of the relationship between man and the physical universe, of what Lear at one point calls 'this little world of man', and to do so without the attempted consolations of received religion. This is not to say that the play's characters have no awareness of the possible existence of metaphysical powers, of forces beyond human knowledge that may nevertheless affect human destiny; some of them do appeal to superhuman powers, but if they pray, the gods they pray to are pagan gods.

The play may be seen as a kind of contrasting and secular companion piece to *Hamlet*, with its Ghost come from a Christian purgatory; its frequent invocations of a single God; its depiction of a King—Claudius—who tries but fails to pray; its arguments about the legitimacy of Christian burial for a suicide—Ophelia; and its eventual summoning of flights of angels to sing Hamlet to his rest.

Lear, on the other hand, in his arrogance addresses pagan, classical gods. In the opening scene, he swears,

> by the sacred radiance of the sun,
> The mysteries of Hecate and the night,
> By all the operation of the orbs
> From whom we do exist and cease to be,
>
> (1.1.109–12)

that he will disown Cordelia. I remember a production in which everyone on stage except Lear himself knelt in awe at the solemnity of this invocation. Later he swears 'by Apollo', to which Kent replies 'Now by Apollo, King, thou swear'st thy gods in vain.' The unsympathetically rational Edmond, the play's most explicit villain, introduces himself with 'Thou, nature, art my goddess.'

The heath on to which Lear is driven by the storm and tempest is a learning place, a sort of tragic inversion of the forest in *As You Like It* or of the desert island of *The Tempest* where men and women may learn the truth about themselves in part through deprivation, so that, as Timon of Athens says, 'Nothing brings me all things.' Slowly during the course of the action Lear is stripped of the trappings of royalty. When he responds to his daughters' heartless claims that he no longer needs a hundred, or 'five and twenty, ten, or five' knights, or even one to serve him, Shakespeare deploys all his rhetorical skills in lines that nevertheless convey a sense of the shifts and turns of Lear's mind swayed by conflicting impulses and passions:

> O, reason not the need! Our basest beggars
> Are in the poorest thing superfluous.
> Allow not nature more than nature needs,
> Man's life's is cheap as beast's. Thou art a lady.
> If only to go warm were gorgeous,
> Why, nature needs not what thou, gorgeous, wear'st,
> Which scarcely keeps thee warm. But for true need—
> You heavens, give me that patience, patience I need.
> You see me here, you gods, a poor old man,
> As full of grief as age, wretchèd in both.
> If it be you that stir these daughters' hearts
> Against their father, fool me not so much
> To bear it tamely. Touch me with noble anger,
> And let not women's weapons, water-drops,
> Stain my man's cheeks. No, you unnatural hags,
> I will have such revenges on you both
> That all the world shall—I will do such things—
> What they are, yet I know not; but they shall be
> The terrors of the earth. You think I'll weep.
> No, I'll not weep. I have full cause of weeping,
> 
> *Storm and tempest*
> 
> But this heart shall break into a hundred thousand flaws
> Or ere I'll weep.—O Fool, I shall go mad!
> 
> (2.2.438–59)

When he learns to identify with others' sufferings he prays more humbly yet still not to a Christian god, addressing the homeless

poor in lines that may speak to us as strongly as they did to his
contemporaries:

> I'll pray, and then I'll sleep.
> Poor naked wretches, wheresoe'er you are,
> That bide the pelting of this pitiless storm,
> How shall your houseless heads and unfed sides,
> Your looped and windowed raggedness, defend you
> From seasons such as these?

> (3.4.27–32)

As Lear says this he is outside the lowliest of dwellings, a hovel,
along with the Earl of Kent, disguised in humble attire; Lear has
sent the only other remaining member of his once impressive
retinue, his loyal and loving Fool, into the hovel in a gesture of
sympathy of which he would once have been incapable. At the end
of his prayer the Fool emerges from the hovel where he has come
upon a representative of the play's parallel plot, Gloucester's once
noble son Edgar, disguised now in exactly the kind of 'looped and
windowed raggedness' as those for whom Lear had been praying,
and playing the role of a mad (Bedlam) beggar that he has
adopted in his desire to serve his father.

The two plots come together here in an absurdist, bitterly comic
scene that brings to a climax the play's concern with the bare
essentials of human life. Lear reveals his obsessive preoccupations
by asking 'Has his daughters brought him to this pass? Couldst
thou save nothing? Wouldst thou give 'em all?' Edgar postures and
cavorts, adopting a scarcely intelligible lingo in his persona of a
mad beggar. If the theatre of Shakespeare's time had permitted
nudity on the stage, Shakespeare might well have called for it
here; it has justifiably been resorted to in more recent productions.
But decorum is preserved; the Fool says 'Nay, he reserved a
blanket, else we had been all shamed.' Lear obsessively continues
in the same vein: 'Nothing could have subdued nature / To such a
lowness but his unkind [unnatural] daughters.' And as Edgar

desperately improvises nonsense in his assumed persona, Lear is provoked to his central reflection on the essential nature of man in relation to the universe:

> Thou wert better in a grave than to answer with thy uncovered body
> this extremity of the skies. Is man no more than this? Consider him
> well. Thou owest the worm no silk, the beast no hide, the sheep no
> wool, the cat no perfume. Ha, here's three on 's are sophisticated;
> thou art the thing itself. Unaccommodated man is no more but such
> a poor, bare, forked animal as thou art. (3.4.95–102)

And he starts to strip off his own clothes: 'Off, off, you lendings! Come, unbutton here!'

Edgar maintains his persona as a mad beggar even more energetically on the entrance with a torch of his father, Gloucester, who tells Lear that he has disobeyed Goneril and Regan's commands to leave him out in the storm:

> Yet I have ventured to come seek you out
> And bring you where both fire and food is ready.
>
> (3.4.142–3)

Lear is declining into full madness. 'His wits begin t'unsettle', says Kent, unrecognized by Gloucester, and the storm rages on as they leave with Lear in a litter for Dover where they expect to find 'welcome and protection'.

Hard upon the climax of Lear's suffering comes Gloucester's, in the horrific episode of his blinding initiated by his son, Edmond, and carried out by the Earl of Cornwall and his wife, Regan. Shakespeare is here confronting his audience with an extreme challenge to their sensibilities that often causes some audience members—myself included—to shut their eyes when it happens. It is the kind of episode that classical dramatists would have been likely to narrate rather than to represent, but Shakespeare wants us to experience its full horror, causing Gloucester himself to compare it to the bearbaiting spectacles in which contemporary audiences delighted: 'I am tied to th' stake, and I must stand the course.' Regan, plucking hairs from Gloucester's beard, takes almost orgasmic pleasure in the spectacle, which so horrifies an anonymous servant that he comes to Gloucester's defence and is killed at Regan's hands. The symbolic nature of the scene is pointed for us when, in immediate response to Gloucester's calling upon his son Edmond to 'enkindle all the sparks of nature / To quite [revenge] this horrid act,' Regan reveals that Edmond himself initiated it: 'Thou call'st upon him that hates thee.' With the son responsible for the father's death, the reversal of the natural order is complete.

The counter-action of the plot comes when Cordelia, leading a French army in the hope of restoring her 'aged father's right' (4.3.28), comes upon him 'As mad as the vexed sea', but having achieved an intermittent kind of serenity on being relieved of the burden of full consciousness. The surreal quality of the play reaches a climax when the disguised Edgar leads his blind father to what he claims is the top of a cliff overlooking the sea at Dover where Gloucester plans to commit suicide by throwing himself onto the beach below. Deluded into believing that he has actually jumped but survived, the old blind man encounters the old mad Lear, crowned with weeds and flowers, in an infinitely touching dialogue which allows Shakespeare to put into the old men's mouths a series of aphoristic, often bitterly satirical and sometimes harshly misogynistic, reflections on their plight and on the human condition more generally which move the onlooking Edgar to the depths: 'I would not take this from report; it is, / And my heart breaks at it' (4.5.137–8).

The play's action winds down as, first, the exhausted Lear falls into a deep and healing sleep, during which, symbolically, 'fresh garments are put on him' and he awakes to sanity and love in the presence of Cordelia and Kent. If Shakespeare had been writing a tragi-comedy the story of King Lear could have ended here. But he had a darker purpose. Lear, restored to sanity and even, as he at first thinks, to life—'You do me wrong to take me out o'th'grave'—is to be subjected to a series of hammer blows of fortune ending only with his death.

The play's closing episodes give great prominence to the sense and sight of the human body as a corpse. Their significance is foreshadowed by Edgar's words to his despairing father: 'Men must endure / Their going hence even as their coming hither.' Regan sickens and dies, poisoned by Goneril. Edgar narrates the story of his father's death. A Gentleman enters carrying the 'bloody knife' with which Goneril has stabbed and killed herself; her body and Regan's are carried on stage in a grim tableau; Lear, whom we had last seen speaking a vision of an eternity in which he and Cordelia would 'sing like birds i'th'cage', carries in her dead body with the lacerating, animal cry of 'Howl, howl, howl, howl!', words which can be interpreted as a series of cries to himself, or as instructions to the onlookers, or as both successively; he seeks in Cordelia's face for signs of life, boasts 'I killed the slave that was a-hanging thee', and, after we have heard that Edmond too is dead, Albany appears to be wrapping up the play by assigning power to the old king:

> ...we will resign
> During the life of this old majesty
> To him our absolute power...
>
> (5.3.274–6)

It looks as if the play will end with an assignment of justice:

> All friends shall taste
> The wages of their virtue, and all foes
> The cup of their deservings.
>
> (5.3.279–80)

But Lear draws attention again to the dead Cordelia in words of great simplicity that may find an echo in the heart of anyone who has ever mourned the loss of someone they love:

> Why should a dog, a horse, a rat have life,
> And thou no breath at all? Thou'lt come no more.
> Never, never, never, never, never.
>
> (5.3.282–4)

And he dies with the words

> Look on her. Look, her lips.
> Look there, look there.
>
> (5.3.286–7)

Does he think he sees signs of renewed life, dying in delusion? Or is he simply overwhelmed with grief at her death? Edgar rounds off the action elegiacally with low-key couplets that summarize the intensity of the human experience that Shakespeare has packed into this play:

> The weight of this sad time we must obey,
> Speak what we feel, not what we ought to say.
> The oldest hath borne most. We that are young
> Shall never see so much, nor live so long.
>
> (5.3.299–302)

Those lines are simply expressed, but the language of *King Lear* is often gritty, sometimes difficult, rarely poetical in an obvious sense, yet also immensely powerful and deeply moving. We remember lines that have a kind of proverbial simplicity: 'I am a man more sinned against than sinning'; 'Nothing can come of nothing'; 'Thou shouldst not have been old before thou hadst been wise'; 'How sharper than a serpent's tooth it is to have a thankless child'; 'When we are born, we cry that we are come to this great stage of fools'; 'Men must endure their going hence even as their coming hither.' And there are scenes too where the language

achieves a kind of divine simplicity, nowhere more touchingly
than when Lear wakes out of madness from sleep in the presence
of Cordelia. At first, in an image of surpassing grandeur, he takes
her to be an angel:

LEAR: You do me wrong to take me out o' th' grave.
  Thou art a soul in bliss, but I am bound
  Upon a wheel of fire, that mine own tears
  Do scald like molten lead.

  (4.6.38–41)

But after that the episode of reunion and mutual forgiveness
between estranged father and daughter is carried through in
language of timeless simplicity, often monosyllabic:

CORDELIA: Sir, do you know me?
LEAR: You are a spirit, I know. Where did you die?
CORDELIA: Still, still, far wide!
[FIRST] GENTLEMAN: He's scarce awake. Let him alone a while.
LEAR: Where have I been? Where am I? Fair daylight?
  I am mightily abused. I should ev'n die with pity
  To see another thus. I know not what to say.
  I will not swear these are my hands. Let's see:
  I feel this pin prick. Would I were assured
  Of my condition.
CORDELIA (kneeling): O look upon me, sir,
  And hold your hands in benediction o'er me.
  You must not kneel.
LEAR: Pray do not mock.
  I am a very foolish, fond old man,
  Fourscore and upward,
  Not an hour more nor less; and, to deal plainly,
  I fear I am not in my perfect mind.
  Methinks I should know you, and know this man;
  Yet I am doubtful, for I am mainly ignorant
  What place this is; and all the skill I have

Remembers not these garments; nor I know not
Where I did lodge last night. Do not laugh at me,
For as I am a man, I think this lady
To be my child, Cordelia.

(4.6.38–63)

The emotional intensity of *King Lear*, its uncompromising
earnestness (to use Hazlitt's word), do not make for easy popularity.
Nahum Tate's softened version, which notoriously gives the play a
happy ending with the peaceful retirement of Lear, Kent, and
Gloucester and the marriage of Edgar and Cordelia, and which
omits the character of the Fool, held the stage (with modifications)
from 1681 to 1839. Later it became customary for directors to give
*King Lear* a prehistoric, Stonehenge-like setting in keeping with
the supposed period of the action, such as may be seen in the DVD
of Michael Elliot's television production starring Laurence Olivier.
But (as with *Macbeth*) the action can successfully be transferred
and even adapted to other settings and societies. Many productions
draw explicit or implicit parallels with modern society. A Leicester
production starring Kathryn Hunter as Lear began and ended in
an old people's home. The Japanese director Akira Kurosawa's film
version, *Ran* (1985), reimagines the daughters as sons. Jane
Smiley's novel, *A Thousand Acres* (1991; filmed 1997), very freely
reimagines the story in terms of the American Midwest. There is
an operatic version (1978), written for Dietrich Fischer-Dieskau by
Aribert Reimann, but projected operas by Verdi and Britten
remained unwritten. *King Lear* is a tough challenge for audiences
and interpreters alike.

# Chapter 9
## *Timon of Athens*

If you go to see *Timon of Athens* you're likely to hear words and to see action that differ greatly from the text of the play as it is printed in any edition you may read. The straightforward reason for this is that the only version of it that has come down to us—and probably the only one that ever existed—is unfinished; an abandoned text written by two dramatists, William Shakespeare and his younger contemporary Thomas Middleton, in a collaboration that fizzled out at a late stage of composition. What we have is a curiously skeletal text, well worthy of resuscitation for its powerful rhetoric, its acute social satire, and the hauntingly beautiful poetry of its later scenes. In the first part of this chapter, I'll write about it in the form in which it is likely to be presented in a reasonably conservative production, without worrying too much about the problems that lie behind it. Later I'll say a bit more about what you'll be confronted with if you read it either as it was first printed or in a modern edition.

The play is a parable that divides conspicuously into two parts. In the first, Timon, an immensely wealthy and prodigally generous Greek nobleman, comes slowly to realize that the men and women he has called his friends are mercenary sycophants who care only for his money. In the second part, bitterly disillusioned, he exiles himself from Athens and lives the life of a hermit, cursing mankind, receiving visits from the people he had previously called friends, and eventually seeking refuge in death.

In the opening scene an unnamed Jeweller shows a Merchant a jewel that he hopes to sell to Timon; a Painter shows a Poet a flattering portrait of Timon; and the Poet summarizes his allegorical poem in which Fortune summons to her a man 'of Lord Timon's frame.' Many men climb after him, but:

> When Fortune in her shift and change of mood
> Spurns down her late belovèd, all his dependants,
> Which laboured after him to the mountain's top
> Even on their knees and hands, let him fall down,
> Not one accompanying his declining foot.
>
> (1.1.85–9)

Though no one is named, this is in effect a summary of the play's action. It is Timon who, initially loved by Fortune, will be abandoned by his dependants when he loses his money.

The first act demonstrates Timon's prodigal generosity. First he offers to redeem a friend from prison by paying his debts, then he gives money to one of his servants to enable him to marry the woman he loves. He pays the Poet, the Painter, and the Jeweller handsomely for their tributes, and invites them and all the company to dine with him. More lords praise him and look forward greedily to receiving more favours. At the subsequent banquet a formal entertainment followed by the distribution of still more gifts provokes yet more obsequious flattery of Timon.

But not everyone joins in the chorus of praise. The cynic philosopher Apemantus jeers at the flatterers and claims there is no such thing as an honest Athenian:

> O you gods, what a number of men eats Timon, and he sees 'em not!
> It grieves me to see so many dip their meat in one man's blood; and
> all the madness is, he cheers them up, too. (1.2.38–41)

But for all his cynicism, there is at any rate one honest Athenian, and that is Timon's steward, Flavius, who reveals to us, though not yet to Timon himself, that his master's fortunes are dwindling. Men to whom Timon owes money start to clamour for repayment. Naively he thinks the people to whom he has been generous will rally round and help him, but in a series of entertainingly satirical scenes they reveal themselves in their true colours. Timon, disillusioned at last, tells Flavius to invite them to another banquet at which, he says, 'My cook and I'll provide.' When the party assembles, his creditors apologize for putting pressure on him, but the scene comes to an ironical climax as *The dishes are uncovered and seen to be full of steaming water [and stones].'* Timon throws water in his guests' faces, turns them out of the house, and departs in fury with words that mark both the turning point of the play and a total reversal of his character:

> Burn house! Sink Athens! Henceforth hated be
> Of Timon man and all humanity!
>
> (3.7.103–4)

In an entertaining coda to the scene, the disconcerted lords return to look for belongings they have lost in the turmoil, and one of them sums up the situation with 'One day he gives us diamonds, next day stones.'

Abandoning Athens, Timon curses the city and all who live there in an impassioned tirade during which, like Lear in the storm, he strips his body bare to the elements, declaring:

> Nothing I'll bear from thee
> But nakedness, thou detestable town;
>
> (4.1.32–3)

He 'will to the woods, where he shall find / Th'unkindest beast more kinder than mankind.'

In the play's second part the patterning is even more obvious than in the first. Initially some of Timon's servants—all Athenians, in

90

spite of his condemnation of the city's inhabitants—speak with
unselfish regret of his fall and condemn the false friends who have
betrayed him. Flavius declares that he will remain faithful: 'Whilst
I have gold I'll be his steward still.'

After this the play is virtually an interrupted soliloquy in which
Timon, now living in poverty in a cave, curses mankind,
especially the inhabitants of Athens, and receives a string of
visitors whom he harangues on—in particular—the corruptive
power of wealth. In the woods, while grubbing for 'roots' on
which to survive, he finds gold. Now it is of no use to him, and he
gives it away as he had previously done, but now as a means of
harming people rather than of doing them favours. He offers gold
to the warrior Alcibiades, who is marching against Athens, as a
help to destroy the city that has rejected both of them, and to a
pair of camp-following whores as a force for damning themselves
and others by fostering the transmission of sexual disease.

The play's most dramatic encounter comes in an exhilaratingly
theatrical scene in which the cynic philosopher Apemantus, who
had earlier cursed Timon's flatterers, now confronts the man who
has had misanthropy thrust upon him as a result of the change in
his fortunes. The pair insult each other with intelligence, energy,
and glee, and Apemantus brilliantly encapsulates Timon's condition
in his comment:

> The middle of humanity thou never knewest, but the extremity of
> both ends. When thou wast in thy gilt and thy perfume, they
> mocked thee for too much curiosity [fastidiousness]; in thy rags
> thou know'st none, but art despised for the contrary. (4.3.302–6)

Timon sees mankind as a parade of beastliness, and what started
as a slanging match ends with the two men hurling stones at each
other.

Reduced to the level of a beast, Timon begins to think of death,
but his sufferings are not over yet. The arrival of a group of thieves

provokes an eloquent outburst in which he imagines all nature preying upon itself:

> The sun's a thief, and with his great attraction
> Robs the vast sea. The moon's an arrant thief,
> And her pale fire she snatches from the sun.
> The sea's a thief, whose liquid surge resolves
> The moon into salt tears. The earth's a thief,
> That feeds and breeds by a composture stol'n
> From gen'ral excrement. Each thing's a thief.
>
> (4.3.438–44)

Misanthropy can scarcely go further; but the reappearance of the steward Flavius reminds us that even among Athenians there are men capable of compassion, love, and loyalty, and that Timon is mistaken in his wholesale denunciation of the human race. Fleetingly and reluctantly he acknowledges this:

> Forgive my general and exceptless rashness,
> You perpetual sober gods! I do proclaim
> One honest man—mistake me not, but one,
> No more, I pray—and he's a steward.
> How fain would I have hated all mankind,
> And thou redeem'st thyself! But all save thee
> I fell with curses.
>
> (4.3.496–502)

And to this 'singly honest man' he gives gold with the cynical injunction that Flavius 'show charity to none.'

At the end of his battle of words with Apemantus Timon had said he was 'sick of this vile world' and advised himself:

> presently prepare thy grave.
> Lie where the light foam of the sea may beat
> Thy gravestone daily.
>
> (4.3.380–2)

The logical outcome of his withdrawal from humanity is a still further retreat into the refuge of death; only extinction can bring him what he wants.

> My long sickness
> Of health and living now begins to mend,
> And nothing brings me all things.
>
> (5.2.71–3)

A strange note of otherworldliness enters his speech as he sends the Senators back to Athens with the message:

> Timon hath made his everlasting mansion
> Upon the beachèd verge of the salt flood,
> Who once a day with his embossèd froth
> The turbulent surge shall cover.
>
> (5.2.100–3)

Timon has no death scene and we don't know who, if anyone, buries him in the grave he has prepared for himself. An illiterate soldier discovers an unexplained gravestone, and makes an impression in wax of the misanthropic epitaph inscribed upon it:

> 'Here lies a wretched corpse,
>   Of wretched soul bereft.
> Seek not my name. A plague consume
>   You wicked caitiffs left!
> Here lie I, Timon, who alive
>   All living men did hate.
> Pass by and curse thy fill, but pass
>   And stay not here thy gait.'
>
> (5.5.71–8)

He takes it back to Athens where Alcibiades speaks compassionately of the dead man, ending a misanthropic play with words of forgiveness:

Is noble Timon, of whose memory hereafter more.

(5.5.84–6)

As I wrote at the start of this chapter, I've tried to describe and to comment on the play without too much emphasis on its textual problems. But in case you would like to know more about the differences between the play as it's likely to be presented in a reasonably conservative production and what you'll read in a modern edition, I'll say a bit more about its textual background.

The only early version that has come down to us is the one published in the first collected edition of Shakespeare's plays, the First Folio of 1623. There is no indication that he had a co-author, but modern scholarship has established beyond reasonable doubt that Thomas Middleton collaborated on it, especially on the satirical scenes. The play was clearly printed from a manuscript that needed a lot of work to be done on it before it could be staged. Stage directions give information that is at odds with what happens in the text. Characters are inexactly identified—lords are given names at some points but referred to only as 'lords' at others, so that it is not clear who should be speaking; the ancient unit of currency known as the talent is worth far more at some points than at others; names occur in variant forms; more subjectively but still conspicuously, the style of writing is very different in some scenes than in others; and the verse is often highly irregular.

The most obvious way in which the play is unfinished relates to the character called Alcibiades. He figures sketchily in the earlier scenes as a warrior on whom Timon bestows bounty. Then after Timon has invited his false friends to the mock banquet we have a scene in which Alcibiades pleads passionately for the life of an unnamed friend who has killed a man in an unexplained manner. The Senate turns down his petition and banishes him. The scene is inadequately worked out and poorly integrated into the overall structure.

Clearly the unfinished state of the text causes problems to the play's theatrical and critical interpreters, but it also leaves them with exceptional freedoms, and in its relatively infrequent revivals the play has been substantially rewritten in the attempt to make it more self-consistent and coherent. Its social satire has appealed to directors who have used updated costumes and settings to emphasize its relevance to the materialistic values of modern society, as in Nicholas Hytner's (2012) production at the National Theatre in which Simon Russell Beale, seen first at a lavish party celebrating the opening of the Timon Wing at a national gallery, ended up as a cardboard citizen wheeling a supermarket trolley amid a mass of urban debris.

# Chapter 10
## *Antony and Cleopatra*

*Antony and Cleopatra* is a great sprawling masterpiece of a play, rich in poetry, vast in imaginative power, in depth of characterization, in psychological penetration, in ironical comedy, and ultimately in tragic grandeur. Its irony results partly from the fact that its central characters invite us not so much to identify with them (as to some extent we may do with Romeo and Juliet, Hamlet, both Othello and Desdemona, and even Macbeth and King Lear), but rather to wonder at them with awed, sometimes amused amazement—marvelling at Antony's desperate infatuation with 'this enchanting queen' from whom he knows he should 'break off'; and at what his follower Enobarbus, who serves as a sort of choric commentator on the earlier part of the play's action, before he deserts Antony, calls Cleopatra's 'infinite variety'. They are larger than life, surprising us, their companions, and sometimes even themselves by the way they behave. When Antony, in a moment of exasperation with Cleopatra, says he wishes he'd never seen her, Enobarbus speaks of her rather as a travel agent might speak to a client who has said he doesn't want to visit one of the wonders of the world: 'O, sir, you had then left unseen a wonderful piece of work, which not to have been blessed withal would have discredited your travel' (1.3.145–7).

Historically the play follows on from *Julius Caesar*, rather as *Henry V* does from *Henry IV Part Two*, and it features some of the same characters as the earlier play, most notably Mark Antony and Octavius Caesar. But the two plays are so different in tone, in verbal style, in treatment of their historical material, and in imaginative impact that it is not easy to think of them together—and they are rarely performed in sequence. The verbal style of *Julius Caesar* is relatively austere, 'classical', controlled, restrained; whereas that of *Antony and Cleopatra* is baroque, extravagant, as different as a painting by Rubens is from an engraving by Piranesi. Its verbal richness means that, although it is immensely theatrical in conception and execution, it has much to offer to readers as well as to theatregoers.

Like *Julius Caesar, Antony and Cleopatra* draws heavily on Plutarch's *Lives of the Noble Grecians and Romans*, not only for its narrative but also for its language in which, in Sir Thomas North's English translation, Shakespeare clearly revelled. Even some of his most consciously poetical passages, such as Enobarbus's famous description of Cleopatra in her barge (painted by Sir Lawrence Alma-Tadema; see Figure 8) are closely modelled on North's prose. The poop, he writes:

> was of gold, the sails of purple, and the oars of silver, which kept
> stroke in rowing after the sound of the music of flutes, oboes,
> citterns, viols, and such other instruments as they played upon in
> the barge. And now for the person of herself: she was laid under a
> pavilion of cloth of gold of tissue, apparelled and attired like the
> goddess Venus commonly drawn in picture, and hard by her, on
> either hand of her, pretty fair boys apparelled as painters do set
> forth god Cupid, with little fans in their hands, with the which they
> fanned wind upon her. Her ladies and gentlewomen also, the fairest
> of them were apparelled like the nymphs Nereides, which are the
> mermaids of the waters, and like the graces, some steering the
> helm, others tending the tackle and ropes of the barge, out of the
> which there came a wonderful passing sweet savour of perfumes

8. 'Cleopatra in her barge'. Sir Lawrence Alma-Tadema (1836–1912).

that perfumed the wharf's side, pestered with innumerable
multitudes of people.

In Plutarch that passage describes how Cleopatra first struck
Antony. Shakespeare places it after he has already portrayed her in
many moods, and turns Plutarch's picturesque prose into an erotic
and poetic vision which gains in effect from being spoken by the
generally sceptical, even cynical Enobarbus:

> The barge she sat in, like a burnished throne
> Burned on the water. The poop was beaten gold;
> Purple the sails, and so perfumèd that
> The winds were love-sick with them. The oars were silver,
> Which to the tune of flutes kept stroke, and made
> The water which they beat to follow faster,
> As amorous of their strokes. For her own person,
> It beggared all description. She did lie
> In her pavilion—cloth of gold, of tissue—

O'erpicturing that Venus where we see
The fancy outwork nature. On each side her
Stood pretty dimpled boys, like smiling Cupids,
With divers-coloured fans whose wind did seem
To glow the delicate cheeks which they did cool,
And what they undid did...
Her gentlewomen, like the Nereides,
So many mermaids, tended her i'th' eyes,
And made their bends adornings. At the helm
A seeming mermaid steers. The silken tackle
Swell with the touches of those flower-soft hands
That yarely frame the office. From the barge
A strange invisible perfume hits the sense
Of the adjacent wharfs. The city cast
Her people out upon her...

(2.2.198–221)

Characteristically of this play, Enobarbus's entranced vision is
followed by a coarse reflection from Agrippa on Cleopatra's earlier
affair with Julius Caesar, by whom she had a son:

Royal wench!
She made great Caesar lay his sword to bed.
He ploughed her, and she cropped.

(2.2.233–5)

*Antony and Cleopatra* is a play of two worlds, Cleopatra's Egypt
and Mark Antony's Rome, and of the links but also of the
contrasts and tensions between them. Its often hyperbolical style
and its narrative and imaginative scope tempt designers to think
of it as a kind of Hollywood epic, calling for visually impressive
sets and large crowd scenes. It's true that from time to time
warriors enter 'with their army', but on Shakespeare's stage this
would have been represented by only a handful of extras, and
in some ways this is a chamber play, with much of the action
confined to small groups of characters and intimate spaces. The

only feature film based on the play, starring Charlton Heston (who is also credited with the script; 1972), has had little success; and the spectacular Hollywood epic *Cleopatra* (1963), starring Richard Burton and Elizabeth Taylor, is not based on Shakespeare's play.

The major characters, however, are certainly larger than life, even though we see them at the troubled ends of their tumultuous careers. And this is very much a play about individual historical characters, about personalities, rather than about the politics in which, as world leaders, they are involved. As a result it is less easily transposed to reflect the period in which it is being performed than are some of Shakespeare's other tragedies. *Julius Caesar* and *Coriolanus* can be related to the politics of later ages, but *Antony and Cleopatra* has only rarely, and not very successfully, been played in modern dress.

Like *Romeo and Juliet*, this is a tragedy of two lovers, but whereas in the earlier play the lovers are teenagers in the throes of first love, here they are a mature and highly experienced couple with many amorous conquests behind them. Antony, who is married to Fulvia at the start of the action, later, to Cleopatra's dismay, marries again—though admittedly his marriage to the cold Octavia is one of political convenience rather than of passion.

In dramatic structure as well as in narrative, too, the plays differ greatly. Fate leads Romeo and Juliet to die together, but the historical narrative requires Antony and Cleopatra to die separately and in very different circumstances, he long (in stage terms) before her, and both of them driven to suicide, though for different reasons. Whereas Juliet's death is accidental, Cleopatra's is self-willed, motivated at least in part by her love for Antony—though also, it might be argued, by self-regard. Romeo kills himself because he believes Juliet to be dead, whereas Mark Antony does so out of military shame as well as because he is made to believe, falsely, that Cleopatra is dead. And whereas the action of *Romeo and Juliet* is confined mostly to

Verona, *Antony and Cleopatra* moves constantly between the opposing poles of Egypt and Rome, the one associated with freedom and sensuality—'I'th'East my pleasure lies', says Antony—the other with self-discipline and austerity. Again like the earlier love-tragedy, *Antony and Cleopatra* is strong on comedy, but here it flecks through the entire action, offering a frequently ironic, sometimes wryly self-critical, perspective rather than, as in the earlier play, falling away as the tragic climax—or climaxes—loom.

The play's fluidity of action is enabled by the structure and conventions of the stages of Shakespeare's time, which, untrammelled with realistic scenery, could switch location in an instant. (Editorial insertion of scene breaks obscures this feature of the text.) And it is facilitated by endless to-ings and fro-ings between Egypt and Rome of messengers and ambassadors carrying news. They shame Antony, besotted in Alexandria, with news of what is going on in Rome and in the large theatre of war in which his forces are fighting without him. They tell tales to Octavius Caesar in Rome about how Antony is revelling in Alexandria while his enemy Pompey's power increases. After Antony has managed to tear himself away from his mistress and return to Rome, he sends messages and gifts to her while she simultaneously sends 'twenty several messengers' to him. But he is driven to infidelity by political need.

A climax comes when a hapless messenger has the unenviable task of telling Cleopatra that in Rome Antony has made a diplomatic marriage with Octavius Caesar's sister Octavia, a lady 'of a holy, cold, and still conversation' (2.6.122–3) whose relationship with her brother is sometimes interpreted as covertly incestuous. After much beating about the bush the messenger comes out with it:

MESSENGER: He's bound unto Octavia.

CLEOPATRA:                For what good turn?

MESSENGER: For the best turn i'th'bed.

CLEOPATRA:                    I am pale, Charmian.

MESSENGER: Madam, he's married to Octavia.

CLEOPATRA: The most infectious pestilence upon thee!

*She strikes him down.*

MESSENGER: Good madam, patience!

CLEOPATRA:                    What say you?

*She strikes him*

Hence, horrible villain, or I'll spurn thine eyes
Like balls before me. I'll unhair thy head,

*She hales him up and down*

Thou shalt be whipped with wire and stewed in brine,
Smarting in ling'ring pickle.

(2.5.58–66)

'I that do bring the news made not the match', says the messenger,
who understandably flees when Cleopatra draws a knife on him.
In a later scene he is brought back to report on Octavia:

CLEOPATRA: Is she as tall as me?

MESSENGER:                    She is not, madam.

CLEOPATRA: Didst hear her speak? Is she shrill-tongued
or low?

MESSENGER: Madam, I heard her speak. She is low-voiced.

CLEOPATRA: That's not so good. He cannot like her long.

(3.3.11–14)

This is great comic writing, a gift to the actor, full of nuance, of
characterful shifts of mood that help to make Cleopatra the
greatest of Shakespeare's comic as well as of his tragic heroines.

It is messengers, too, who bring news, after Antony has torn himself
away from Rome and returned to Cleopatra, which precipitates
the sea-battle of Actium at which Antony is ignominiously
defeated; messengers who negotiate with Caesar on behalf of the
lovers and then return with the information that Caesar will make

terms with Cleopatra only if she sends Antony away or has him
executed. It is a messenger who secures Cleopatra's agreement
'to lay [her] crown' at Caesar's feet and who is sentenced to a
whipping when Antony finds him kissing Cleopatra's hand; and
who tells Enobarbus, who has defected from Antony, that his
master has magnanimously sent his possessions after him.
Messengers tell Antony on Cleopatra's instructions that she has
killed herself and come, too late to save him, to reveal that this
was one of her manipulative tricks; messengers bring news to
Caesar of Antony's suicide and ask the victorious Caesar on
Cleopatra's behalf what he intends to do with her after he has
taken her captive. They reassure her that he will treat her well
while deceptively putting her under armed guard; and finally they
tell her that he intends to lead her in triumph to Rome and to
exhibit her to the people. The use of messengers, some named,
some not, creates a sense of continual movement and urgency,
giving impetus to an action that might otherwise seem episodic
and plotless.

Like *Romeo and Juliet* this is a double tragedy, but here the lovers
die not together but apart in both space and time. Mark Antony
dies before Cleopatra does, while believing the false news that
she has killed herself and looking forward to an eternity of bliss
with her:

> Where souls do couch on flowers we'll hand in hand,
> And with our sprightly port make the ghosts gaze.
> Dido and her Aeneas shall want troops,
> And all the haunt be ours.

(4.15.51–4)

The play's double climax can cause a feeling that it has to start all
over again after coming to an apparent end, but the later stages of
the action are sustained partly by unexpected shifts of plot and by
the fact that Cleopatra remains gloriously unpredictable. The
dying Antony is hauled up to her on the upper level of the stage

which represents her monument, and dies a noble death,
provoking her to lament it in cosmic terms:

> O see, my women,
> The crown o'th'earth doth melt. My lord!
> O, withered is the garland of the war.
> The soldier's pole is fall'n. Young boys and girls
> Are level now with men. The odds is gone,
> And there is nothing left remarkable
> Beneath the visiting moon.
>
> (4.16.64–70)

And she falls down, leading her attendants to suppose that she too
has died. But she recovers, prepares to bury Antony, and looks
forward to her own death 'after the high Roman fashion.' Caesar
finds it hard to believe that Antony has died:

> The breaking of so great a thing should make
> A greater crack.
>
> (5.1.14–15)

and weeps for his old enemy. When he hears that Cleopatra has
retreated to her monument and seeks to know what he intends to
do with her, he promises to treat her honourably. But his messenger
Proculeius tricks her and prevents her from committing suicide
on the spot lest she be taken captive to Rome and displayed
in humiliation.

When Dolabella, yet another messenger from Caesar, comes to
guard her she speaks a final, great, idealized tribute to Antony,
envisioning him as an all-conquering, prodigally generous
demi-god who could have existed only in the imagination:

> His legs bestrid the ocean; his reared arm
> Crested the world. His voice was propertied
> As all the tunèd spheres, and that to friends;

> But when he meant to quail and shake the orb,
> He was as rattling thunder. For his bounty,
> There was no winter in 't; an autumn 'twas
> That grew the more by reaping. His delights
> Were dolphin-like; they showed his back above
> The element they lived in. In his livery
> Walked crowns and crownets. Realms and islands were
> As plates dropped from his pocket.
>
> (5.2.81–91)

And, learning that Caesar means to lead her in triumph, she kneels to him in apparent abjection, and hands over a note which, she says, lists all her possessions. But again she has lied. Her treasurer, Seleucus, reveals that she has kept back as much as she has admitted to possessing, and Cleopatra turns on him with all her old vehemence: 'I'll catch thine eyes / Though they had wings.' She knows that if she accompanies Caesar to Rome he will parade her before jeering crowds:

> Antony
> Shall be brought drunken forth, and I shall see
> Some squeaking Cleopatra boy my greatness
> I'th'posture of a whore.
>
> (5.2.214–17)

And she begins to prepare to die by her own hand. Urged on by thought of the indignities to which Caesar will subject her if he leads her captive to Rome, she prepares for death with incomparable dignity:

> I am fire and air; my other elements
> I give to baser life.
>
> (5.2.284–5)

But Shakespeare has still one more surprise for us. A 'rural fellow' whom she has commissioned to bring her deadly asps which will be the instruments of her death enters claiming to bring merely figs, and in a bizarre episode of clownish humour wishes her 'joy of the worm.' But as he leaves, her maid brings in her 'robe, crown, and other jewels' and Cleopatra, applying an asp to her arm, dies in transcendent but still ironical glory:

> Peace, peace.
>> Dost thou not see my baby at my breast,
>> That sucks the nurse asleep?
> CHARMIAN:                O, break! O, break!
> CLEOPATRA:  As sweet as balm, as soft as air, as gentle.
>> O Antony!
> *She puts another aspic to her arm*
>>> Nay, I will take thee too.
>> What should I stay—
> *She dies*
> CHARMIAN:  In this vile world? So, fare thee well.
>> Now boast thee, death, in thy possession lies
>> A lass unparalleled.
>
>>>>>>> (5.2.303–10)

Just as Antony had looked forward to an eternity of bliss with Cleopatra, so she too sees death as the culmination, but not the end, of their relationship:

>>> methinks I hear
>> Antony call. I see him rouse himself
>> To praise my noble act. I hear him mock
>> The luck of Caesar, which the gods give men
>> To excuse their after wrath. Husband, I come.
>>
>>>> (5.2.278–82)

So for the lovers this tragedy ends, like a comedy, with the hope of marriage—but beyond the grave.

# Chapter 11
## *Coriolanus*

For what we believe to be his last tragedy (though not, presumably, by intention), Shakespeare turned once again to Ancient Rome, and to Thomas North's translation of Plutarch's *Lives*. Once more he chose to write about a heroic warrior whose personal fate is bound up with that of his nation, as he had with Titus Andronicus and Macbeth, but once again he avoided any sense of repetition either in terms of the personality of his protagonist or in the structure and tone of his drama. And as in, especially, *Antony and Cleopatra*, he depicts a unique, psychologically complex individual rather than a central character who may be regarded as an everyman figure.

The poetic style of this play is implicitly characterized by T. S. Eliot in the opening lines of his poem 'Coriolan':

> Stone, bronze, stone, steel, stone, oakleaves, horses' heels
> Over the paving.
> And the flags. And the trumpets. And so many eagles.

Characteristically it is knotty, harsh, austere, intellectually rigorous, and resolutely unlyrical—poles apart from that of *Antony and Cleopatra*. But as usual the dialogue is leavened with humour, sometimes conscious on the part of the speakers, but no less frequently oblique and ironical. The satirical element in the play is indeed so prominent that Bernard Shaw, with characteristic love of paradox, ironically referred to this as 'the greatest of Shakespeare's comedies.'

Coriolanus was a great Roman warrior of the 5th century BC, known originally, and referred to in the earlier scenes of the play, as Caius Martius (or Marius.) 'Coriolanus' is a 'cognomen'—an honorific addition—a name given to him because as a young man, as the play graphically shows, he conquered the town of Corioles, south of Rome. (It's a bit like calling Field Marshal Montgomery 'Viscount Montgomery of Alamein', after the Battle of El Alamein). Corioles was in the territory of the Volscians, whose capital was Antium.

The play is a political as well as personal drama that can easily be seen to relate to national issues, especially to relationships between rulers and the people they rule, at many later periods of history; it is also a profound psychological study of a complex individual caught up in a web of difficult personal relationships that reflect basic human situations.

Shakespeare's fascination with the interior life of a hero fixated on his mother was clearly stimulated by Plutarch's opening description of him and of the paradoxes in his nature, which reads rather like a school psychiatrist's report:

> Caius Martius, whose life we intend now to write, being left an orphan by his father, was brought up under his mother, a widow, who taught us by experience that orphanage bringeth many discommodities to a child, but doth not hinder him to become an honest man, and to excel in virtue above the common sort: as they are meanly born wrongfully do complain that it is the occasion of their casting away, for that no man in their youth taketh any care of them to see them well brought up, and taught that were meet. This man also is good proof to confirm some men's opinions, that a rare and excellent wit untaught doth bring forth many good and evil

things together, like as a fat soil bringeth forth herbs and weeds
that lieth unmanured. For this Martius' natural wit and great heart
did marvellously stir up his courage to do and attempt notable
acts. But on the other side, for lack of education, he was so choleric
and impatient, that he would yield to no living creature: which
made him churlish, uncivil, and altogether unfit for any man's
conversation.

Shakespeare depicts his hero—or should we say 'anti-hero'?—in
relation mainly to three groups of characters. These are the people
of Rome, the people of Corioles, and his family. The people of Rome
are represented primarily by their tribunes, Sicinius Velutus and
Junius Brutus—elected leaders of the people who exert a powerful
and not entirely benevolent influence over them. The people of
Corioles—the Volscians—are led by Tullus Aufidius, Coriolanus's
chief enemy with whom he nevertheless has a love-hate relationship
that can easily be interpreted as homo-erotic. And the chief
representative of his family is, significantly, not his wife, Virgilia,
but his mother, Volumnia.

Like *Julius Caesar*, the play opens with a lively scene portraying
citizens, here depicted in a state of rebellion because they blame
the greed of the patricians, the ruling class of Rome, for a famine
brought about by a shortage of corn. (In this Shakespeare seems to
have been reflecting topical and local issues of his time.) The
common people see Caius Martius (the future Coriolanus) as their
'chief enemy', 'a very dog to the commonalty', and their discussion
rapidly centres on him and on an argument about the underlying
motives for his services to his country, demonstrated by his
successes in warfare, which one of them defines not as genuine
patriotism but rather as a mixture of personal pride and a desire
'to please his mother', thus introducing a psychological issue
central to the play.

The aristocrat Menenius, a close friend of Martius and his family,
who nevertheless, one of the citizens admits, 'has always loved

the people', attempts with good-humoured tact to pacify the
citizens and to persuade them that the patricians have been acting
in their best interests. However, when Martius comes on the
scene he does nothing to serve his own cause by haranguing them
at length as 'dissentious rogues' whom, if he had his way, he would
slaughter *en masse*. He has just announced with contempt that
the city authorities have appointed five tribunes, led by Junius
Brutus and Sicinius Velutus, to represent the people's interests
when news comes that the Volscians, the enemies of Rome, are
in arms and marching against the city. They are led by Tullus
Aufidius who, says Martius, is 'an enemy I am proud to fight.' The
complex, love-hate relationship between these two warriors will
dominate the rest of the play's action.

So far we have seen Martius at his worst. Shakespeare's need to
depict what Plutarch calls 'his courage to do and attempt notable
acts' is responsible for an original structural feature of this play.
Usually, as in *Richard III*, *Julius Caesar*, and *Macbeth*, battle
scenes represent the climax of a play's action, but here Shakespeare,
needing to demonstrate Martius's greatness as a warrior in
contrast to his total failure as a diplomat—a characteristic that has
often helped the play seem relevant to later ages in which great
soldiers have failed signally to make the transition from warfare
to peace—shows him at his best in battle scenes that occur early in
the play's action, in which he does amazing feats of courage. His
general, Cominius, rewards him with the gift of his own horse and
by conferring upon him the honorific name of 'Coriolanus'.

In the meantime Shakespeare has shown us another of the play's
principal groups of characters, Coriolanus's family. It is not too
much to say in Freudian terminology that Coriolanus has a
fixation on his mother, Volumnia. We first see her in the company
of his wife, Virgilia, and their young son, another Martius
in character as in name—we hear of him tearing a butterfly to
bits—in a domestic scene (invented by Shakespeare) which
probingly portrays Roman values with satirical force. In her first

speech Volumnia boasts that she has always been pleased to let her son 'seek danger where he was like to find fame.' When Virgilia asks how she would have felt if he had been killed, she replies 'Then his good report should have been my son...had I a dozen sons, each in my love alike, none less dear than thine and my good Martius', I had rather had eleven die nobly for their country than one voluptuously surfeit out of action.' His wife, distressed, tries to leave, but Volumnia insists she remain while she fantasizes about an encounter between the two leaders in a speech which includes its own directions for illustrative gesture and action:

> Methinks I hear hither your husband's drum,
> See him pluck Aufidius down by th'hair;
> As children from a bear, the Volsces shunning him.
> Methinks I see him stamp thus, and call thus:
> 'Come on, you cowards, you were got in fear
> Though you were born in Rome.' His bloody brow
> With his mailed hand thus wiping, forth he goes,
> Like to a harvest-man that's tasked to mow
> Or all or lose his hire.
>
> (1.3.31–9)

Virgilia, understandably, quails:

> His bloody brow? O Jupiter, no blood!
>
> (1.3.40)

This sets Volumnia off again:

> Away, you fool! It more becomes a man
> Than gilt his trophy.
>
> (1.3.41–2)

In this scene Shakespeare is clearly concerned to portray the values of an alien society. What kind of people, he seems to be asking, were they who behaved like this? What were the values by

*Coriolanus*

which they lived, and into what dilemmas did their values force them? What can cause a great hero so to despise his fellow men that he cannot behave with common civility to them? Why should a great soldier be such a total failure as a statesman?

Shakespeare follows this with a vivid depiction of Martius in action, cursing his soldiers as they retreat before the enemy, threatening that if they don't renew their efforts he will turn on them himself, and urging them to follow as he fights his way into the gates of the enemy city. But they refuse, the gates close, and Martius is shut in. All seems to be lost, and the general Titus Lartius speaks what is virtually an epitaph on Martius, but he re-enters, 'bleeding, assaulted by the enemy', and after more skirmishes, bloodier than ever, embraces his general Cominius with a tribute that, significantly to the psychological subtext of this play, links warfare with love-making:

> O, let me clip ye
> In arms as sound as when I wooed, in heart
> As merry as when our nuptial day was done,
> And tapers burnt to bedward!
>
> (1.7.29–32)

Martius renews the attack in hope of engaging in direct combat with the Volscian leader, Aufidius, and declaring hatred for one another they come face to face. Aufidius survives only because 'certain Volscians' come to his help, and 'Martius fights till they be driven in breathless'. This provokes in Aufidius a declaration of enmity so intense that he says he will stoop to any means of conquering Martius:

> Where I find him, were it
> At home upon my brother's guard, even there,
> Against the hospitable canon, would I
> Wash my fierce hand in's heart.
>
> (1.11.24–7)

This is the last time we see Aufidius until, much later, Coriolanus, turning against his native Rome, will seek him out in his own home and offer to serve the man who has been his sworn enemy. Martius takes the tributes paid to him by his soldiers, including the conferring of the name Coriolanus, with an ill grace, and slopes off to wash his face.

Shakespeare has firmly established Coriolanus's greatness as a warrior, but now he seeks advancement to the high office of consul, and, in spite of all the efforts of his mother and his friends to persuade him to behave diplomatically, so conspicuously fails to conceal his contempt for the citizens that, egged on by the self-seeking and manipulative tribunes, they turn against him; accused of seeking to behave tyrannically, he loses control and curses them:

> The fires i'th' lowest hell fold in the people!
>
> (3.3.71)

Unsurprisingly, the internal dissension in Rome between Coriolanus and the citizens whom he so despises reaches such a pitch that they banish him from the city, to which he responds with unparalleled vehemence, declaring that he in turn banishes them:

> You common cry of curs, whose breath I hate
> As reek o'th' rotten fens, whose loves I prize
> As the dead carcasses of unburied men
> That do corrupt my air: I banish you.
> And here remain with your uncertainty.
>
> (3.3.124–8)

And he stalks resoundingly off with

> Despising
> For you the city, thus I turn my back.
> There is a world elsewhere.
>
> (3.3.137–9)

This is the play's first major turning point, and one that Shakespeare negotiates with supreme psychological subtlety. Abandoning Rome and entering enemy territory—Antium, capital city of the Volscians—Coriolanus, 'in mean apparel, disguised and muffled', meditates on mutability.

> O world, thy slippery turns! Friends now fast sworn,
> Whose double bosoms seems to wear one heart,
> Whose hours, whose bed, whose meal and exercise
> Are still together, who twin as 'twere, in love
> Unseparable, shall within this hour,
> On a dissension of a doit, break out
> To bitterest enmity. So fellest foes,
> Whose passions and whose plots have broke their sleep
> To take the one the other, by some chance,
> Some trick not worth an egg, shall grow dear friends
> And interjoin their issues. So with me.
> My birthplace hate I, and my love's upon
> This enemy town. I'll enter. If he slay me,
> He does fair justice; if he give me way,
> I'll do his country service.

(4.4.12–26)

The unnamed 'he' is, of course, Coriolanus's prime enemy, Aufidius. When they meet, Coriolanus offers to join him in taking his revenge against his 'cankered country' Rome or, if Aufidius dares not do this, to present him his throat to cut in revenge for all the harm he has done to the Volscians. Aufidius responds in a speech of great psychological acuity which demonstrates how close hatred can be to love, and which fully justifies the homo-erotic interpretation that modern actors often bring to the roles:

> Let me twine
> Mine arms about that body where against
> My grainèd ash an hundred times hath broke,
> And scarred the moon with splinters.

*(He embraces Coriolanus)*

> Here I clip
> The anvil of my sword, and do contest
> As hotly and as nobly with thy love
> As ever in ambitious strength I did
> Contend against thy valour. Know thou first,
> I loved the maid I married; never man
> Sighed truer breath. But that I see thee here,
> Thou noble thing, more dances my rapt heart
> Than when I first my wedded mistress saw
> Bestride my threshold.
>
> (4.5.107–19)

And he tells that he has nightly:

> Dreamt of encounters 'twixt thyself and me—
> We have been down together in my sleep,
> Unbuckling helms, fisting each other's throat—
> And waked half dead with nothing.
>
> (4.5.124–7)

They go off in comradeship.

The security of a now peaceful Rome is disturbed when rumour comes that Coriolanus has joined with Aufidius and that they are marching against the city, devastating all the land that lies in their way, and in another episode satirizing the Roman citizens they are shown claiming that 'though we willingly consented to his banishment, yet it was against our will' and declaring 'I ever said we were i'th'wrong when we banished him.'

A scene between Aufidius and his Lieutenant shows that the Volscian leader, though full of admiration for Martius's valour, is astutely aware of the politics of the situation, and he delivers a balanced assessment of his enemy-turned-comrade such as could have come from an objective observer and that serves as a second epitaph for him even though he is not yet dead:

> I think he'll be to Rome
> As is the osprey to the fish, who takes it
> By sovereignty of nature. First he was
> A noble servant to them, but he could not
> Carry his honours even. Whether 'twas pride,
> Which out of daily fortune ever taints
> The happy man; whether defect of judgement,
> To fail in the disposing of those chances
> Which he was lord of; or whether nature,
> Not to be other than one thing, not moving
> From th' casque to th' cushion, but commanding peace
> Even with the same austerity and garb
> As he controlled the war: but one of these—
> As he hath spices of them all—not all,
> For I dare so far free him—made him feared,
> So hated, and so banished. But he has a merit
> To choke it in the utt'rance. So our virtues
> Lie in th' interpretation of the time,
> And power, unto itself most commendable,
> Hath not a tomb so evident as a chair
> T'extol what it hath done.

(4.7.33–53)

He concludes by revealing that, in spite of all of his protestations of admiration and even love for Coriolanus, he still regards him as an enemy:

> When, Caius, Rome is thine,
> Thou art poor'st of all; then shortly thou art mine.

(4.7.56–7)

Coriolanus's failure to 'dissemble with [his] nature' and give way to the citizens—as his mother thinks he should—his moral integrity,

116

in other words—paradoxically requires him to pretend hatred for those he loves. He listens to the entreaties first of Menenius, who calls Coriolanus both his lover and his son, but is sent away unrewarded.

> This man, Aufidius,
> Was my beloved in Rome; yet thou behold'st.
> (5.2.92–3)

But then comes the play's most emotionally loaded scene (5.3), in which Coriolanus has to listen to the pleas of his mother, his wife, and his son—as well as his wife's friend, Virgilia—as they plead on behalf not only of themselves but of Rome too (Figure 9). It is a long scene, in which Coriolanus struggles to deny his own nature, to keep up the pretence that he has been able to renounce all personal as well as national loyalties. The sight of his family forces him to a truer self-recognition:

> I melt, and am not
> Of stronger earth than others.
> (5.3.28–9)

He tries to distinguish between personal and national loyalties, hoping he can show affection for his family without having to renounce his enmity to Rome, but his mother eloquently insists on the need for compromise. If he conquers Rome, he conquers her.

The long speeches of this scene demonstrate Shakespeare's mastery of literary rhetoric in the service of drama. And the stage direction in which they culminate as the supplicants finally kneel before him demonstrates even more eloquently his mastery of theatrical effect. Coriolanus 'holds her by the hand, silent' in a moment of submission which is also a profound moment of self-examination and an acceptance of his fate:

> O mother, mother!
> What have you done? Behold, the heavens do ope,

*Coriolanus*

CORIOLAN
FLECHI
PAR SA MERE

9. Volumnia pleads with Coriolanus to have mercy on her, on her family, and on Rome. C. N. Cochin, engraving of 1789.

> The gods look down, and this unnatural scene
> They laugh at. O my mother, mother, O!
> You have won a happy victory to Rome;
> But for your son, believe it, O believe it,
> Most dangerously you have with him prevailed,
> If not most mortal to him. But let it come.
>
> (5.3.183–90)

He knows he has consigned himself to death. But he knows too that he has done the right thing, seeking no longer a god-like aloofness from natural emotion but accepting instead the full burden of his own humanity: the need to acknowledge relationship. At the same time he accepts the inevitability of his own death. 'But let it come' is the counterpart in this play to Hamlet's 'The readiness is all', and to 'The ripeness is all' in *King Lear*. But it is the final paradox of the mother–son relationship in this play that Volumnia, calling for a full expression of her son's love for her, brings about his death. Thus closely are love and hate related.

*Coriolanus*'s concern with the relationship between the personalities of national leaders and the fate of their countries has given it topicality at many later periods of history. In the 17th century, Nahum Tate, adapting it as *The Ingratitude of a Commonwealth*, remarked on its 'resemblance to the busy faction of our time', alluding to the alleged Popish Plot against Charles II. More recently, politically motivated productions, not always on the same side of the fence, have been given. In Paris in 1932 it provoked right-wing demonstrations, in Germany during the 1930s school editions drew admiring parallels between Coriolanus and Hitler, whereas shortly afterwards a Moscow production is said to have portrayed Coriolanus as 'a superman who had detached himself from the people and betrayed them.'

In 1963 the Berliner Ensemble presented a version based on an unfinished adaptation by Bertolt Brecht which reduced Martius's stature as both warrior and statesman. Günter Grass's play known in English as *The Plebeians Rehearse the Uprising* (1966) shows Brecht rehearsing his version of *Coriolanus* as news gradually reaches the theatre of risings within Berlin against the imposition by the party on the government of new labour regulations. Perhaps in reaction, John Osborne in 1973 published a 'reworking' called *A City Calling Itself Rome* which adopts an emphatically right-wing stance. In London, a National Theatre production of 1984 directed by Peter Hall with Ian McKellen as Coriolanus drew parallels with Thatcherite Britain. Hall had previously directed a less topically orientated production at Stratford-upon-Avon in 1959 with a central performance of blazing power and witty irony from Laurence Olivier. The only feature film version, directed by and starring Ralph Fiennes, with Vanessa Redgrave as Volumnia (2011), brilliantly and excitingly updates the action in a shortened version of the text which relates it to issues of modern warfare.

# Epilogue: why might we enjoy tragedies?

In offering a guided tour of Shakespeare's tragedies I have had to assume that my readers are interested in the form itself. This may seem slightly odd. Theatre is generally regarded as a form of entertainment. Why, we may ask, should one pay good money to subject oneself to displays of misery, cruelty, suicide, assassination, murder, and even cannibalism? Many responses to this question could be suggested; the simplest is that it posits an excessively limited view of the function of theatre—as if it existed only to amuse.

But more nuanced responses are possible too. One is that Shakespeare's tragedies, like most good plays, tell dramatic, well-shaped stories that carry us with plot-driven impetus through a series of interconnected events to a conclusion that fulfils the expectations that have been aroused during the course of the action. Another is that they do so in language that can entrance sympathetic listeners (or readers) with its lyricism, its rhetorical force, its complex variety, its power to suggest individuality of character, its subtle interrelationships that create a sense of individual identity for each play, and that can have aphoristic pungency. It is relevant too that Shakespeare constructs his tragedies in a manner that frequently provides an ironic, comic perspective on the characters and the way they behave. The fusion

of tragedy with comedy, anathema to neo-classical critics
(see Chapter 5, pp. 55–6), creates a sense of truth to the diversity
and complexity of human experience which a narrower focus
would forbid.

Perhaps central to the appeal of Shakespeare's tragedies
(and others) is that they give us a sense of sharing in and
facing up to the ultimate realities of human existence; of the
intermingling in our lives of joy and sorrow, of love and
hatred, of conflicting impulses of kindness and cruelty; of the
inevitability of death and of the pathos of human endeavour
to mitigate its terrors; of the mystery inherent in the human
condition. Here tragedy has some of the quality of religious
ritual, giving us a sense of participating, in the company of fellow
human beings of whatever era, in the effort to assimilate the
harsher elements of human life and of the mitigations and
consolations that can accompany us on the journey to death,
even of the possibility that, as Hamlet puts it, there may be
'something after death.'

This possibility, however, fills Hamlet with dread rather than
with hope, making him willing to 'bear those ills we have /
Rather than fly to others that we know not of.' Shakespeare's
comedies often suggest the possibility, or at least the hope, of
reunion and resurrection. In his tragedies, however, although, as
we have seen, Mark Antony can envisage a (distinctly pagan)
afterlife 'Where souls do couch on flowers' (Chapter 10, p. 103),
more frequently Shakespeare seems to see death as, at best, an
eternal rest—oblivion—or at worst a state in which, as Claudio
puts it in *Measure for Measure*, we 'lie in cold obstruction' and rot;
or, no more invitingly, in which we:

> reside
> In thrilling region of thick-ribbèd ice;
> Imprisoned in the viewless winds,

And blown with restless violence round about
The pendent world;

(3.1.122–6)

Shakespeare's tragedies offer no easy answers to the dilemmas that beset us, but they may stimulate and console us by making us ponder eternal issues and helping us to participate in a sense of shared humanity.

# References

All Shakespeare quotations are from Stanley Wells and Gary Taylor (eds), *Works* (Oxford: Oxford University Press, 2005, 2nd edn).

## Chapter 2: *Titus Andronicus*

James Agate, *Brief Chronicles* (London: Jonathan Cape, 1943), 188
Frank Kermode, *Shakespeare's Language* (London: Penguin Books, 2000), 8
J. C. Trewin, *Shakespeare on the English Stage 1900–1964* (London: Barrie and Rockliff, 1964), 235–6

## Chapter 3: *Romeo and Juliet*

Ellen Terry, *The Story of My Life* (London: Hutchinson, 1908), 208
Edwin Wilson (ed.), *Shaw on Shakespeare* (London, 1962), 246
Evans: quoted in James Agate, *The Selective Ego*, ed. Tim Beaumont (London: Harrap, 1976), 36 (the critic was W. A. Darlington)

## Chapter 5: *Hamlet*

Voltaire: adapted from the translation in H. H. Furness's New Variorum edition of *Hamlet* (Philadelphia, 1877, 2 vols), vol. 2, p. 381
'the wiser sort': Gabriel Harvey, cited in *The Shakspere Allusion Book* (Oxford: Oxford University Press, 1932, 2 vols), vol. 2, p. 56

Gilbert: Stanley Wells (ed.), *Nineteenth-Century Shakespeare Burlesques* (London: Diploma Press, 1977, 5 vols), vol. 4, p. 249

Hall: quoted in Stanley Wells, *Royal Shakespeare* (Manchester: Manchester University Press, n. d. (1977), 27

## Chapter 6: *Othello*

Rymer: Brian Vickers (ed.), *Shakespeare: The Critical Heritage* (London: Routledge and Kegan Hall, 1974, 2 vols), vol. 2, pp. 25–59

Brander Matthews (ed.), *The Dramatic Essays of Charles Lamb* (London: Chatto and Windus, 1891), 188

Samuel Taylor Coleridge, *Shakespearean Criticism*, ed. T. M. Raysor (London: Chatto and Windus, 1960, 2nd edn, 2 vols), vol. 1, p. 42

'defile the stage': cited by Bernth Lindfors, *Ira Aldridge: The Early Years: 1807–1833* (Rochester, NY: University of Rochester Press, 2011), 257

## Chapter 8: *King Lear*

William Hazlitt, from *Characters of Shakespeare's Plays* (1817), in Jonathan Bate (ed.), *The Romantics on Shakespeare* (London: Penguin, 1992), 394

Johnson: Arthur Sherbo (ed.), *Johnson on Shakespeare* (New York: Yale University Press, 1968, 2 vols), vol. 2, p. 704

## Chapter 10: *Antony and Cleopatra*

Plutarch: T. J. B. Spencer (ed.), *Shakespeare's Plutarch* (London: Penguin, 1964), 201

# Select filmography

Filmed performances of all the tragedies are available in the BBC television series (1978–85), and most are also available in DVD versions of live performances from the Royal Shakespeare Company, Shakespeare's Globe, and other sources. I list below some of the best of the feature films of these plays.

*Coriolanus*, directed by Ralph Fiennes, 2011

*Hamlet*, directed by:

> Laurence Olivier, 1948
> Grigori Kozintsev, 1964 (in Russian)
> Franco Zeffirelli, 1990
> Kenneth Branagh, 1996

*Julius Caesar*, directed by Joseph L. Mankiewicz, 1953

*King Lear*, directed by:

> Peter Brook, 1971
> Michael Elliott, 1983 (for television)
> Grigori Kozintsev, 1969 (in Russian)
> Akira Kurosawa, 1985 (as *Ran*, in Japanese)

*Macbeth*, directed by:

> Orson Welles, 1948
> Ramon Polanski, 1971
> Justin Kurzel, 2015

*Othello*, directed by:

> Orson Welles, 1952
> Stuart Burge, 1965
> Oliver Parker, 1995

*Romeo and Juliet*, directed by:

> Franco Zeffirelli, 1968
> Baz Luhrmann, 1996 (as *William Shakespeare's Romeo + Juliet*)

*Titus Andronicus*, directed by Julie Taymor, 1999 (as *Titus*)

# Further reading

## Editions

Annotated editions of single works with informative scholarly and
critical introductions are available in the Oxford World's Classics
and other series. The Penguin Shakespeare offers accessible
introductions and studies of the plays in performance.

## Reference

Margreta de Grazia and Stanley Wells (eds), *The New Cambridge
Companion to Shakespeare* (Cambridge: Cambridge University
Press, 2010)

Andrew Dickson, *The Globe Guide to Shakespeare* (London: Profile
Books, 2016)

Claire McEachern (ed.), *The Cambridge Companion to Shakespearean
Tragedy* (Cambridge: Cambridge University Press, 2005)

Michael Dobson and Stanley Wells et al. (eds), *The Oxford Companion
to Shakespeare* (Oxford: Oxford University Press, 2001; 2nd
edition, revised, 2015)

## Language

Frank Kermode, *Shakespeare's Language* (London: Allen Lane,
2000)

Russ McDonald, *Shakespeare and the Arts of Language* (Oxford:
Oxford University Press, 2001)

## Life

Recommended biographies of Shakespeare include:

S. Schoenbaun, *A Compact Documentary Life* (Oxford: Oxford University Press, 1977)

Park Honan, *Shakespeare: A Life* (Oxford: Oxford University Press, 1998)

Lois Potter, *The Life of William Shakespeare* (London: John Wiley, 2012)

*Shakespeare* by Bill Bryson (London: Atlas Books, 2007) is a popular short life

## Life and afterlife

Stanley Wells, *Shakespeare: For All Time* (London: Macmillan, 2002)

Russell Jackson, *Shakespeare and the English-Speaking Cinema* (Oxford: Oxford University Press, 2014)

## Sources

Robert S. Miola, *Shakespeare's Reading* (Oxford: Oxford University Press, 2000)

Kenneth Muir, *The Sources of Shakespeare's Plays* (London: Methuen, 1977)

T. J. B. Spencer (ed.), *Shakespeare's Plutarch* (Harmondsworth: Penguin, 1964)

## Criticism

A. C. Bradley, *Shakespearean Tragedy: Lectures on Hamlet, King Lear, Othello, Macbeth* (Oxford: Oxford University Press, 1904, frequently reprinted)

Adrian Poole, *Tragedy: A Very Short Introduction* (Oxford: Oxford University Press, 2005)

Jonathan Bate (ed.), *The Romantics on Shakespeare* (London: Puffin, 1992)

Edwin Wilson (ed.), *Shaw on Shakespeare* (1961)

## Theatre

There are helpful volumes on most of the tragedies in the series
'Shakespeare in Performance', published by Manchester University
Press.

Stanley Wells (ed.), *Shakespeare and the Theatre: An Anthology of
Criticism* (Oxford: Oxford University Press, 1997)

# Publisher's acknowledgements

We are grateful for permission to include the following copyright material in this book.

Excerpt from 'Coriolan' from *Collected Poems 1909–1962* by T. S. Eliot. Copyright 1936 by Houghton Mifflin Harcourt Publishing Company. Copyright © renewed 1964 by Thomas Steams Eliot. Reprinted by permission of Houghton Mifflin Harcourt Publishing Company and by Faber and Faber Ltd as the publishers. All rights reserved.

The publisher and author have made every effort to trace and contact all copyright holders before publication. If notified, the publisher will be pleased to rectify any errors or omissions at the earliest opportunity.

# Index

## W

Walter, Harriet  33, 74
Warner, Deborah  20–1
Welles, Orson  33, 65, 74
Westall, Richard  xiv
White, Willard  65
*Wilhelm Meister* (Goethe)  53

*Winter's Tale*  4
*Witch, The*
     (Middleton)  68
Wright, John Massey  28

## Z

Zeffirelli, Franco  30, 45